This Book May Be My
LASTER

And Also My
WORSTER

Which Is Baddera
Than AWFULER

This Book May Be My
LASTER

And Also My
WORSTER

Which Is Baddera Than
AWFULER

Bernice Zakin

Copyright © 2011 by Bernice Zakin.

Library of Congress Control Number: 2014916553
ISBN: Hardcover 978-1-4990-7051-4
Softcover 978-1-4990-7052-1
eBook 978-1-4990-7050-7

All rights reserved. No part of this book may be reproduced or transmitted in any form or by any means, electronic or mechanical, including photocopying, recording, or by any information storage and retrieval system, without permission in writing from the copyright owner.

Any people depicted in stock imagery provided by Thinkstock are models, and such images are being used for illustrative purposes only.
Certain stock imagery © Thinkstock.

This book was printed in the United States of America.

Rev. date: 10/22/2014

To order additional copies of this book, contact:
Xlibris
1-888-795-4274
www.Xlibris.com
Orders@Xlibris.com
540117

PREVIOUS BOOKS WRITTEN BY BERNICE ZAKIN

POETRY

From Bad To Verse Or The Verse Is Yet To Come

Cool Verse And Hot Doggerel

OTHER BOOKS

If You Take The Train Home Where Do You Put It?

At Last Inanimate Objects Speak Up

Alphabetically Alliterative Collection Of Corny Compositions

Grandma Has A Tale

I Went, I Saw, I Ate

Stuff From Out Of My Head

Stuff I Forgot To Remember

This Book May Be My Laster And Also My Worster Which Is Baddera Than Awfuler

DEDICATION
(A repeat from previous books but always relevant)

Always to the memory of my late husband Albert Zakin
To my children Nancy and Jeff, and Barbi and Ken
All my grandchildren: Lizzie and Jon, Carly and Peter,
Andy and Dana, David and Susan, Kenny and Alyson and
Debbie and Michael
Finally my great grandchildren: 13 in number and they
are not to be slighted, but are too numerous to name
individually
(I do know their names however!)

AGAIN

Well here I am again after I practically took an oath that I would not write another book. So okay I'm a Liar!

Actually I am still not positive that this current amount of writing will evolve into a complete volume, but because several ideas keep bouncing around in my noodle, what else can I possibly do.

I can't just leave them to muddle up my brain. If I did then my head would be very messy so out of sheer desperation I decided to write an additional book.

Frankly I don't believe I should be pleased about having another publication because I doubt if Elise will be particularly happy to type all of it as I will admit that my handwriting is almost impossible to decipher and it will be very much a strain on her eyes. Then too I am not so sure Marcus will be willing to purchase all my printing ink.

Besides which, I am already exhausted just thinking about all the Costco trips I will have to make in order to buy more yellow pads, typing paper and pens.

The sad thing is that I can never go to Costco for just these "necessaries". It is impossible to leave there without toilet tissue, Kleenex, paper towels, napkins, books, some food stuff, and an occasional article of clothing, plus lunch, therefore the cost of such visits are humongous!

In any event herein is my new book. However if none of you care to read it I really don't mind. You can pretend you read it or you can even tell me you liked it. Actually I personally didn't like it so much myself. But what the heck, here it is anyway.

P.S. Hopefully it will be fun for any possible old readers and who knows, I may also develop some new ones along the way. (I actually have two readers!)

NOTHING IN PARTICULAR BUT IMPORTANT

This entire book is the result of the collaborative efforts of the Xlibris staff who did the actual printing and handled all the technicalities of its production and publication.

And let's not forget Elise Alarimo who transcribed all of the material and conducted the business end so ably. She made the many telephone calls, filled out various forms and arranged the entire table of contents, etc and was incredibly involved throughout this entire procedure. All in all she has been a positive treasure.

Finally, I (Bernice) designed and drew the book's front cover as I did with all 9 of my other books and of course I am totally responsible for the literary contents.

CONTENTS

A Bubby Micie 17
A Caring Friend 18
A Conversation With Bernice 19
A Numerical Solution 21
A Really Bad Day 23
A Sad Tale 26
A Strange Thing 28
A Thought Worth Contemplating 31
A Toothsome Episode 32
Aging Or Not 34
Alas Poor Obama 35
All In The Family 36
A.M. Getting Up 38
An Accident Incident 39
An "Udder" Book? 41
An Unusual Incident 42
Anything Worthwhile In This Book Is Purely Coincidental 43
Autumnal Activities 44
Belly Russe 45
Big Is Beautiful 46
Birthday Blues 47
Blank 48
"Body" Parts 49
Celebration 51
Celebrations 53
Clichés 54
Common Expressions 57
Confused 59
Cut It Out 60
Date Book 62
Disease 63

Does This Give You The Willies?	64
Double Trouble	66
Embarassing Moments	67
Everyone Else Loved The Movie But I Was Bored	68
Eye See!	69
Fear Of Heights	70
Flash!	72
Food For Thought?	74
Hair Today Gone Tomorrow	76
Halloween At The Home	77
Happy Birthday To Far Away Debberino	79
Harken	80
Hello	81
Hey Hey Doc	82
Hi Jesus!	83
Home Is Where You Have To Pay Rent	84
Hope	86
How I Changed My World And When It Started	88
How To Be A Good "Skate"	93
How To Be The Teacher Of This Class?	95
How To Link Out	97
How To Vote	99
Ideas In The Night	101
If And Where To Snack	102
Ill Annoying	104
Il Pleut	106
Insomnia	108
I Think I Am Listless	109
I've Got You Under My Skin	110
I Wonder	112
Joan	113
Late For The Date	114
Latitude	116
Longevity - Long May It Live!	117
Lost And Found	119
Mail	122
Mason	123
Mauled At The Mall	124
Me	126

Me And Them	127
Mistaken Identity	129
My Apartment	130
My Bathroom Memories	134
My Doctor	137
My Kids	138
My Life Is An Open Book	139
My New Life	141
My Problem	142
My Resume	143
My Sighs For My Size	145
"New" Is The "New"	146
News Flash	148
Nobody Knows Anybody	149
No Fly Zone	150
No More	151
No Thank You I'd Rather Stay Home	152
Off They Go	154
Once Upon A Time	156
"On The Other Hand"	159
Over Heard	161
Preventive Medicine	162
Republican Rogues	164
Secrets	165
She Knows It All	170
Showers	171
Sordid Revelations	172
Telling Tales	174
The American Obsession With Firearms Invades Our Conversations	175
The Battle Is On	176
The Big Day	177
The "Bridge" Of Sighs	179
The Card Room	181
The Couple	183
The Early Me	185
The Emperor Has No Clothes Or The Bully In The School Yard	186
The End?	187
The "Inside" Story	189
The Old Neighborhood	191

The Real Me	193
The Seat Of Luxury	195
The Secret Is Out	196
The Whiner	197
Things Are Not Always What They Seem To Be Initially	199
This Is A Ferry Tale	201
This Is A Poem	203
Time Flies	204
Time Marches On	205
Tommy Toe	206
To Think	207
Trayvon	208
Two Of A Kind	209
Vacation Clothes Woes	210
Viewpoint	212
Water Water Everywhere	213
What's In A Name?	214
What To Do?	216
Where Did They Go?	217
Where Do Or Did They Go?	218
Where Is It One?	220
Where Is It Two?	222
Which Is He?	223
Whine Not	224
Who Is It? (A Tragic Situation!)	225
"Who Lives In Those Cute Little Houses"?	226
Why Worry	228
Winner Take "Hall"	229
Winter Woes	230
Word Problems	231
"Write" Or Wrong	233
You Can't Take It With You	234
Finally – Finis	236

A BUBBY MICIE

It's absolutely true. I had a bubby which most Americanized Jewish people now call a great grandmother, and I recall mine quite vividly.

As to the word Micie, this in no way refers to my great grandmother as being part of a race of varmints. In no way was she part mouse. I believe it is just a common expression of the Yiddish variety which indicates a "grandma story".

At any rate my bubby was a tiny lady who wore a wig and was very pleasant. She was also the former wife of 4 husbands, although not at the same time, and she died falling down a flight of stairs enroute to a wedding (not hers). I also think she missed the ceremony.

Actually I only met her once when I was about 8 years old and she came to visit my maternal grandmother, (her son was my maternal grandfather).

I remember being quite impressed to learn that she was 94 years old, which seemed terribly aged to me at that time. Today of course I am not aghast at that number of years as I even have a neighbor aged 106 who still plays bridge.

My bubby most definitely did not play bridge although she probably wore one in her mouth attached to some teeth.

Relatively speaking (no pun intended), I consider myself to be very fortunate to have had a great grandmother despite the fact that today I am one myself.

A CARING FRIEND

My good friend Elaine Winick called me recently and asked why my voice sounded so strange. I told her that I had a "Hoarse" in my throat.

Elaine whose sense of humor is similar to mine, then asked me what kind of "Horse" it was.

Naturally I replied "A colt!"

A CONVERSATION WITH BERNICE

A conversation with me can be very enlightening. A person can soon find out everything about me as you will now discover.

For instance

1. Question- Bernice how would you like to have dinner with me at Peter Lugers, the steak is truly divine?

2. Answer - I don't eat meat

3. Question - Bernice would you care to go to that new fish restaurant in Roslyn one night?

4. Answer - I don't really like fish

5. Question - My car is being fixed so would you mind driving to Stresa's restaurant in Manhasset one evening?

6. Answer - I don't drive at night

7. Question - Would you care to go to the Ballet this Saturday. I believe "Swan Lake" is on the program?

8. Answer - I saw it many times.

9. Question - I just read the best book "Me Before You" would you care to borrow it.

10. Answer - I read it.

11. Question - I hear you are having a birthday next week. How old are you going to be?

12. Answer - I can't remember and it's none of your business.

13. Question - By the way for which of the two candidates for mayor do you intend voting.

14. Answer - Yes

A NUMERICAL SOLUTION

There presently exists in our hemisphere a species of people who are called "Mothers", and these individuals have a great deal in common with a group termed as "their children".

Now these "mothers" in some instances are forced to relinquish their function as successful arbiters in the business world in order to assume their new roles as household persons.

At that time they also have what we refer to as complete control over the bodies and minds of their little ones i.e. "the children".

This includes defevering them and tending to them during periods of childhood diseases such as measles and chicken pox, etc.

Also this covers the feeding, clothing and bathing of them, plus attending to all of what "the children" consider to be their important needs.

This care is totally without recompense. Motherly services are free of charge, mostly out of what we call the goodness of their maternal hearts.

As a result, motherly solicitude is generally responsible for producing adults who are able to take their rightful places in society, and to hopefully become citizens in good standing.

Alas however! this is not always so. Sometimes these individuals (whom we occasionally call "Moms") can fail miserably and become derelict in their execution of motherly duties, and in that case "the children" do not always become exemplary, law abiding, honorable people.

Therefore it is logical to assume that "mothers" per se do not necessarily achieve their objectives.

So sometimes another body of people known as "fathers" have to be included in the successful rearing of their small ones.

Thus! Numerically speaking "two" in some instances are better than "one".

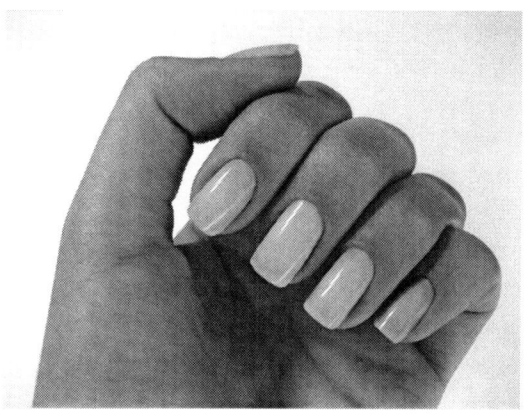

A REALLY BAD DAY

Sunday mornings are generally my favorite time of the week. I can just lounge around and do practically nothing else except watch my special TV programs, which is a most enjoyable pastime.

However this past Sunday morning was a total disaster and I will now explain why I have made this very sad statement.

You see I have a manicure every Saturday and because I have extremely long nails which extend far beyond my nail beds, I usually have my manicurist apply a very glamorous silver colored polish to enhance my nails, and I must say they normally look very nice all week.

But on this particular Sunday to which I just referred, I unfortunately banged my finger (the one next to my pinky) against a table and the nail swung back and completely cracked open at the nail bed.

Naturally this destroyed my manicure and I was left with a dangling nail as well.

So what did I do? I did what any supposedly smart person would do.

I opened my kitchen gadget drawer and looked for some crazy glue to repair my nail damage.

At first I was not able to find any, but then I spied a brand new tube which was encased in a heavy plastic wrapping. This proved to be almost impossible to open so I finally had to snip it apart with a pair of scissors.

I briefly glanced at the warning words on the cut wrapping which indicated what to do if any of the glue spilled on something valuable and could not be removed. Then I threw the wrapping into my waste can.

But the tube seemed to be unable to open even after I tugged and tugged. Suddenly though I remembered that there was another tube of crazy glue in another drawer which I immediately removed from that drawer and fruitlessly tried to open it. Although after squeezing and squeezing it too would not dispense any of the glue, until in desperation I cut off the entire top of the plastic tubing which usually made the glue ooze out. This worked so I squirted it out. But then it got all over my lovely white plastic cutting board which was covering and protecting my black slate counter top.

That's when mayhem set in! There was so much glue oozing out that the tube was soon empty and I had to mop up all the residue. So I grabbed some Kleenex from the container on my counter and started wiping. Well! That was a big mistake. The Kleenex attached itself to all my fingers on both hands and the more I wiped the more mess there was both on my cutting board and ME! We were both covered with gooey glue, and Kleenex and it was all sticking! Except that it never got on my ruined fingernail. So I still had a dangling nail! Then since there was no more glue left in that tube, I decided to go back to the original red tube which finally yielded its gooey glue in big clumps that squirted out fast and furiously. Again it was all over the cutting board which was now almost completely ruined, although I did manage to swish my finger with the dangling nail into the mess and Voila! At last I had an attached nail!

This saga was still continuing because then I tried to remove some of the stuck on glue which was now all over the cutting board and seemingly continuing onto my slate counter therefore I got some Q-Tips which I thought would be able to solve my problem - No! It didn't because the Q-Tips did not have wooden ends. They had plastic ones which kept bending so they were of no use and the glue was apparently stuck forever.

Ingeniously I remembered the warning words on the red tube's original wrapping, so I then went to the waste can to retrieve it and read the blessed wording about removing stuck on glue. It said "use nail polish remover" which I did but not before getting stuck to the waste can's lining paper with the still wet glue on my fingers, which of course were still stuck with lots of Kleenex pieces. But at least I had a reattached nail.

However I finally realized why the manufacturers of Crazy Glue gave it its name - it's because it can really drive you CRAZY!!!

P.S. I was so busy wiping up and trying to get unstuck that I was unable to listen to any of my TV programs. So much for lovely Sundays!

A SAD TALE

So this is my story

I was in third grade and I was very smart. So smart that the teacher didn't want me in the <u>lower</u> third grade any more so she put me in the <u>upper</u> third grade class. So there I was, very lonesome. I didn't really know anybody in my <u>upper</u> third grade class until the time came for me to go to the <u>lower</u> fourth grade where I knew everybody, but then I was still very smart so the new teacher put me in the <u>upper</u> fourth grade, and again nobody I knew was in this class.

I was also too smart again even though I felt dumb, therefore that teacher became very sorry for me and because I didn't know many people in her class either, she decided that I should go to <u>lower</u> fifth grade, where this new teacher was about to teach long division, but since I got the chicken pox and missed a good many school days, I never learned long division and never got to know many of the other students.

So there I was, lonesome again, not so smart anymore and absolutely ignorant about long division. Oh I forgot! I never learned fractions either, I missed those too. Boy was I dumb!

The result was that I ultimately graduated from grade school and went on to high school and college. But I now need an accountant, a full time bookkeeper and a tremendous abundance of money so I don't have to worry about knowing how to count or do any math at all.

Actually I don't believe it is necessary for me to be smart either, or have a lot of friends. I just have to be rich!

A STRANGE THING

Emily Boxer, a young American student was in London on a semester abroad and was enjoying it tremendously.

She dutifully attended her classes every day, but also enjoyed an exciting social life as well, which included making friends with many students from all parts of the world.

In addition, simply touring around London was a favorite activity. Indeed at least once a week she would wander into different parts of the city. She particularly liked to visit the many beautiful art galleries that were so prevalent in London.

Actually Emily was hoping to enter the art world someday herself as she was quite talented artistically, and had very high hopes of becoming a future Picasso, Matisse, or some other equally well known art notable (in her future life).

One day however, when she passed a small gallery that she had never visited before, she impulsively entered it and poked around at length, admiring the many beautiful canvases that graced the walls. In fact a particularly lovely portrait immediately caught her attention.

The longer she gazed at it the more she was convinced that it was a likeness of her own deceased mother as a young girl. But how could that be?

She knew that her mother had never been abroad, so she presumed she was either completely mistaken as to the identity of the painting's subject, or that perhaps the artist had been an American and had somehow painted her mother long ago in the United States.

At any rate on a whim Emily approached the nearby salesperson and asked if he knew the name of the lady in the painting, and explained to him that the resemblance to her mother was so great. She also wanted to know if the canvas was for sale and how much it would cost.

The young man said he really didn't know but would ask the gallery owner to speak to her.

A that point an elderly gentleman from the back of the gallery came over and peered at Emily in a very unusual way.

First he said that the painting of which he was the actual artist was not for sale, and then explained that the woman in the portrait had been his wife many years ago. Then he hesitantly asked "is your name Emily"?

Emily of course was shocked and queried "how do you know my name?" The man abruptly sat down on a nearby bench, wiped his suddenly perspiring forehead and then said "I believe I'm your father".

This statement was like a bolt from the blue and Emily was stunned beyond words. She could not understand what the man was saying.

As far as she knew her mother had never been married to anyone other than her father, who was also deceased, and besides she was shocked to believe that the man whom she always considered to be her father could possibly not be her dad after all.

Emily who was an only child had always had a very secure and happy childhood. There were many photographs of her and her parents from her infancy, and nothing in her life was anything other than completely normal, with the same mother and the same father, therefore any other scenario was unthinkable.

But the older gentleman went on to explain. He said "my name is Emile. You were named for me when you were born. However at that time I was a very poor artist living in New York where your mother and I met fell in love and got married".

"Then shortly after you were born I was recruited into the army during the Vietnam War and was sent abroad. Almost immediately I was severely injured and had complete memory loss and was declared to be deceased".

"Consequently your mother believing she was a widow remarried". By this time, Emile further explained how he had tried desperately to find Emily and her mother when he finally regained his memory some years later but although he contacted numerous government agencies for information, the fact that he did not know her mother's present name made it impossible so he finally had to give up all hopes of finding them. He also mentioned that he never remarried and obviously had no other children.

Emily was immeasurably moved by Emile's sad tale and was finally convinced that his story was true when he showed her a worn and tattered photograph of her mother, Emile and Emily together when she was an infant.

The upshot of this strange story was that Emily finally realized that even though she had presumed she was now an orphan, that in fact she had discovered a new and seemingly wonderful father. This was a boon indeed which promised the assurance of a loving relationship and future ahead for both of them.

A THOUGHT WORTH CONTEMPLATING

In my last book I wrote what I intended to be a humorous essay that explored the possibility of reversing the role of man versus animal, i.e. if we were to become dogs for instance, and they in turn were to become human.

At first I really thought this was a comical idea, however it recently led me to consider this supposed occurrence from an entirely different approach, which is our treatment of animals as pets.

And after seeing the movie "Twelve Years A Slave", I suddenly realized that we as pet owners were actually enslaving them.

Yes, we play with them, feed them, walk them, etc. But are they truly free creatures? Don't we really keep them under our control? Are we not in fact enslaving them? Isn't our ownership something they cannot prevent? Isn't this actually a sort of bondage?

Is this what God intended (that is if there really is a God)? Isn't ownership and controlling another being, whether human or animal a most appalling thought?

What is the answer?

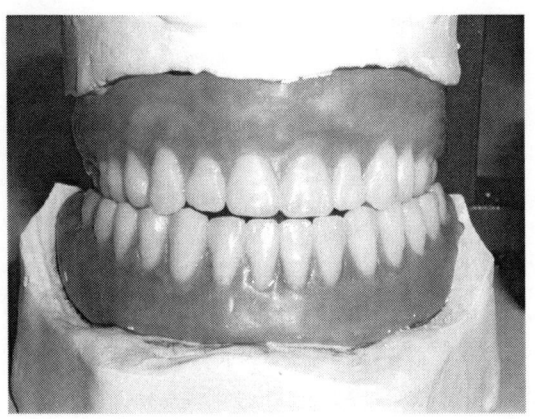

A TOOTHSOME EPISODE

Sometimes strange things happen to me and I generally forget them, but since my memory is occasionally fairly accurate I feel compelled to relate a particular incident that occurred many years ago when I attended a Broadway mystery play.

It was a boring kind of afternoon as the performance was poorly acted and definitely not believable. It did not appeal to me at all. In fact I hated it. However it appeared that most of the audience thought otherwise, as everyone around me seemed to be clapping madly.

I was embarrassed to leave but on the other hand I found it hard to concentrate on the dull scenes I was watching.

Therefore I fidgeted and squirmed in my seat and started reviewing the items in my handbag instead of looking at the stage.

While I was peering at my various belongings, I inadvertently dropped my bag, and thus I had to poke around under my seat to find it. Then to my horror I found myself fingering a set of false teeth! which was startling, scary and eerie!

At that time I didn't know whether this occurrence was part of the script or just happenstance.

Nevertheless at that point I was really hating the show and so I left the theater! I also imagine that the owner of the teeth had done the very same thing.

AGING OR NOT

So we all are living longer and if so, what difference does it make?

Is our hair underneath our dye jobs none the less grey? Don't the bulges that are now squeezed within the confines of our girdles or whatever contraption or coverage we wear still exist? And isn't thin hair just as good as or better than no hair?

Also when people of our vintage keep saying to us "you look great". Isn't it because they too are living longer and can't see too well or that they really don't mean it?

And what about memory loss? Isn't that of no importance, who cares about the past as long as we can live in the present and future.

Then too shouldn't we be grateful for the innovations that either exist now or are about to be discovered ultimately? Or will our children be the only beneficiaries of our futures?

In the long run as I see it, nothing really matters so long as we are healthy and happy now.

ALAS POOR OBAMA

Alas poor Obama
Whom the Reps can't abide
They castigate him with epithets snide
They say he's a Kenyan
But mostly a black
And some of them claim
That he's even on "crack"
So what's his salvation?
What can the guy do?
As the next thing you know
They'll say he's a "Jew"

ALL IN THE FAMILY

I am very proud to say that I have an extremely brilliant great grandchild.

Now you may think that I am being unduly boastful. However in the following sentences I can absolutely prove to you that I am telling the unmitigated truth.

To further explain how I know this, I will have to clarify how children attempting to enter any preschool in New York City are first exposed to the rigors of the required testing method.

These little kiddies at the tender ages of 2-3 are awkwardly positioned in tiny little chairs facing a severely countenanced grown up who is sitting in a large chair.

This grownup generally bombards these little tykes with a series of questions and their answers will then determine whether their intelligent responses will qualify them for acceptance in a worthy preschool.

When the time came for my little great granddaughter to demonstrate her intellectual ability at her age of 2.5 years, she was asked if she could identify the name of an item that was red, had big wheels and a loud siren.

In most cases the average child would probably say "a fire engine" but not my little one. She was much more imaginative and clever in her response which was "a kangaroo".

Of course the person interviewing her did not have enough of a creative mind to accept her definition and therefore, Mason (my little one) was not voted worthy of acceptance at one particular school, at which her father, aunts, and paternal grandmother had been former students, and also I might add, generous yearly monetary donors.

Unfortunately, the creative genius of this child was not recognized. However as her totally unbiased great grandmother I thoroughly realized how correct and impressive her response was, and I am sure you all probably agree with me.

A.M. GETTING UP

Wake
Stretch
Yawn
Kvetch
Shower
Dress
Look in mirror
What a mess
Call a friend
Make a date
Why oh why
It's who I hate
Drink some juice
Then some tea
That's it
Have to pee!

AN ACCIDENT INCIDENT

Ooh-Oh-Ouch! Carol Simmons almost fell and then briskly rubbed her ankle, which really hurt from being accidentally kicked by a clearly contrite, handsome young man. He helped her to regain her balance and kept asking if he could be of further assistance, and when Carol said no, he finally insisted on her having a cup of coffee with him at a nearby small restaurant in order to relax after her accident.

He was very insistent and seemingly so trustworthy that she decided to accept his invitation.

After a most pleasant interlude in the coffee shop Carol found herself slightly besotted by this charming young man, whose name was Edmond Prentiss, and when he invited her out on a real date she was eager to accept.

This date led to several other very pleasant evenings, and pretty soon Carol felt she had a steady boyfriend, until one evening when he had taken her home after their dinner together, she realized that her wallet was missing. Edmond was most helpful in trying to backtrack with her to figure out where she might have lost it, in the powder room of the restaurant in which they had dinner? Under the dinner table? In the taxi that took them back to her apartment? They checked everywhere to no avail.

At any rate two days later Edmond called her to say that his firm was unexpectedly sending him to Brazil on business, and he was leaving the very next day for probably about 4 months but he promised to write once he got settled.

Carol was quite disheartened and realized how much she would miss him, but of course she understood that his business commitment was necessary.

Six months later, after never having heard from him, Carol just happened to be in the same neighborhood in which she had originally met Edmond and realized that a young man about 6 people ahead of her, stuck his foot out in front of the girl next to him causing her to fall and then he solicitously helped her up.

At that point Carol recognized the man as Edmund, and hid in the doorway near her so she was able to see him befriend the young lady in the same manner in which he had originally met Carol.

She also saw that he persuaded that girl to accompany him into a conveniently situated coffee shop, just as he had done with Carol so many months ago.

It was then that she came to the conclusion that Edmund was a scam artist and that no doubt this young lady would soon lose her wallet as well as her heart.

AN "UDDER" BOOK?

At one time I thought I would write an "udder" book even tho the title of this one belied my ever doing so.

Also it wasn't because I once lived in "cowtown" (Fort Worth, Texas).

It had nothing to do with the fact that I had been "cowtowed" by anyone or anything.

I never had a "cowlick". My head is very neat but not filled with anything impressive.

I am often in a an "udder" state of confusion but I am not a "coward" and I don't drink milk!

AN UNUSUAL INCIDENT

Recently I had a most unusual conversation in a Palm Beach greeting card store.

I was attempting to purchase a few toys for my visiting grandchildren and noticed that there were no such items on the store shelves where formerly there had been an abundance of them.

I lamented this situation to the lady behind the counter and instead of the answer I expected from her, I heard a decisive comment from a customer behind me.

She said "that's because people are giving their children away".

Snidely I queried – where do they send them?

Her answer was "The Caribbean!"

ANYTHING WORTHWHILE IN THIS BOOK IS PURELY COINCIDENTAL

I have an enormous confession to make "yea and verily". This is the truth. I do not write anything worthwhile. In fact I am not actually a writer.

I am simply a reader. I read how to read books, scandalous magazine articles, the bills that arrive in my mailbox, billboard signs and the directions written on medical forms as to how to take prescriptions ordered by a doctor.

I am also familiar with certain driving signs - like turn right at next light, stop signs, and deer crossings.

Beyond this I do not read too much. I find that reading is a strain on the eyes. Then too, it sometimes causes a person to think, which is a strain in the brain, and it can also prod a person into making book purchases which is definitely a strain on wallets and bank accounts.

Therefore I suggest that none of you should read this book as that might really be a strain.

AUTUMNAL ACTIVITIES

This is the time of year when I get myself checked out medically from one end to the other.

So far this season I've been to the offices of five doctors and still have four to go.

Mind you I am a really healthy person and this has been attested to by the five docs I've already visited.

However the next four may have different diagnoses and conclusions. At any rate the following weeks will tell the tale.

By the way each of the five I've already seen are quite unique. Three of them have captivating senses of humor, one is extremely intellectual and the last one is most genial and kind. All in all I don't think I could have chosen a more accommodating group.

Let's hope the next four will deserve my accolades as well. They certainly will if they declare me to be fit as a fiddle and THEY BETTER DO THIS!

BELLY RUSSE

The Russky named Vladmir Putin
Has a diet I don't think is gluten.
But he thinks he's a czar
So he eats caviar
While Russian funds I think he's lootin'

And then he drinks lots of vodka
But never eats Jewish type lotka
As he's anti the Jews
And all gays he'll abuse
Tho I hear he can dance the
Kazatska!

BIG IS BEAUTIFUL

I was listening to the radio in my car the other day, and caught the tail end of a talk show on which a man (presumably a comedian) related a story about when he was enroute to a gig he was recently hosting.

This is what I heard him say "Wendy Williams was coming out of the elevator I was entering and boy! She had the biggest "entourage" I've ever seen! Then he said "there were about 20 people following her".

Naturally I originally misinterpreted what I thought he meant because I'd heard that Wendy had undergone extensive breast augmentation.

Thank heavens he continued his statement so that it was clarified, and I realized what he actually meant. Although the original part of his statement was even more true.

BIRTHDAY BLUES

Psst! It's a secret
Not many folks know
On whose birthday cake
The candles will blow

She's a lady whose hobby
Is flowers and plants
And of course in her gardens
There never are ants

She's great playing bridge
Plus canasta as well
Tho as far as golf goes
She's not really "swell"

But she's fun and looks lovely
Though the truth must be told
That we're talking 'bout Cheryl
And the fact is she's old-d-d-d-d!!!

BLANK

This morning I woke up and there was no "there" there. When I looked out the window I discovered that I lived in a blank cocoon. The fog was so thick that I was completely cut off from the world and all I had left was my apartment.

I used to have friends whose windows I could peer into from my building and into theirs which was across from mine, but now those people have disappeared. This is really sad to say because I used to enjoy their company and now since my world has become so small - it is very lonesome.

Also I previously enjoyed looking at what formerly was the blue sky with pretty white fluffy clouds that moved along in varying shapes - now where there used to be an "up there" there is <u>nothing,</u> nada. So I am forced to just be "me" alone.

I do hope everything where there used to be an "out there" will come back, and <u>soon</u> - as I am not sure that I really like "just me"!

"BODY" PARTS

(He's an "ass")
A "frame" of reference
I lost my "voice"
My "hands" are tied
Put your "shoulder" to the wheel

(She's an "ass")
Keep a "breast" of the situation
Keep a "head" of the game
My "heart" wasn't in it
Don't be so "nosey"

(They are both "asses")
She has a "finger" in every pie
I really got an "earful"
Put your money where your "mouth" is
A "hair"ey situation

(Don't be an "ass")
Keep your "eye" on the ball
"Hip hip" hooray!
Don't "palm" it off on me
Stop "elbowing" in

(What an "ass")
"Thumbs" up
A "figure" of speech
No "bones" about it
"Toe" the mark

(I never saw such an "ass")
Made it by the "skin" of my "teeth"
None of your "lip"
Stop "ribbing" me
Don't "muscle" in

(Don't be such an "ass")
"Knuckle" down Winnsocky
A slip of the "tongue"
He's a lame "brain"
I can't "stomach it"

(You're an "ass"!)
You can't get "blood from a stone"
This place is a real "joint"
Any "body" home?

(You really are an "ass")
The horses are "neck" and "neck"
The U.S. "Naval" Academy
You're in the "Arm"y now

(They are all "asses")
That's pretty "cheeky" of you
I have a "gut" feeling
This is the main "artery" into Manhattan
Look it up in the "appendix"
(Up yours A---------------!)

CELEBRATION

This is it folks - a time to celebrate! My <u>car</u> is a lovely beige 2001 Lincoln L.S. With 4 doors, window wipers, and even a place to store little coins, if needed for parking. AND! This car is now about to embrace its <u>13th</u> year of existence.

Therefore (as the proud owner) I expect to have <u>car</u> mitzvah for it. The place will be "<u>Ca</u>rdini's restaurant in New Hyde Park. The time and date - soon!

We can't fit all our guests in one car so we have to have a <u>car</u> pool.

Also a beautiful red <u>car</u>pet will be laid in front of <u>Ca</u>rdini's to welcome our lovely guests whom I hope will be wearing <u>car</u>digan sweaters to <u>fit</u> the occasion (and of course <u>them</u>).

My center pieces will be varitoned <u>car</u>nations and delicious <u>car</u>amels will be scattered on the table.

This Book May Be My Laster And Also My Worster Which Is Baddera Than Awfuler

Also since it is now so close to the Christmas holidays, I expect to have a group of <u>Ca</u>rolers singing during the party. Then too there will possibly be some members of a local opera company as well and they will offer melodies from "<u>Ca</u>rmen".

After a lavish luncheon, <u>ca</u>rafes of coffee and tea will be served and of course many different <u>car</u> bonated drinks.

This will hopefully be one heckova gathering because it will also indicate that my <u>car</u> will soon be retired - Yes! My garage man recently said that it is definitely time for my Lincoln to re <u>tire</u>!

CELEBRATIONS

This is going to be an amazing and unusual holiday season. One that will not reoccur for 79 thousand years, according to historians.

The reason is that both Thanksgiving and Hanukah will fall on the same day, which is a most incredible situation. So how do we deal with it in order to treat both holidays equally?

Do we circumcise the turkey before roasting it?

Do we put yamakas on our yams?

Do we put 8 candles on the dining table?

Or do we serve Hanukah <u>pan</u>cakes as opposed to serving our Thanksgiving cakes in <u>pans</u>?

This certainly is going to be a mixed up day so I guess we'll just to say Happy everything!

CLICHÉS

Did you ever wonder how clichés came to pass and what some of them actually mean?

In my odd moments I seem to think of unusual things, and pondering about this particular thought led me to make my own explanations, so I am listing several of them in the next few paragraphs.

1. "Put your money where your mouth is". This cliché possibly occurred when a person who was too poor to buy a wallet, and had no pockets, finally resorted to placing his money in his mouth for safe keeping.

2. "Keep a stiff upper lip". In today's world, fashionable ladies who are on the "getting older" cusp, generally go to a plastic surgeon, who does a little botoxing on their mouths. This makes their lips puff up and eliminates crinkles. Youth then arrives in no time at all.

3. "Call a spade a spade". This naturally refers to older bridge players who are not sure of their ability to see properly, and therefore sometimes mistakenly believe that a club ace is a spade ace. What a very bad situation this can be if they need the 4 points of the ace in their spade bid.

4. "<u>Bite off more than you can chew</u>" greedy people who are inclined to stuff themselves, often choke on an oversized chunk of food and soon it is lodged immovably in the back of their throats. If they have a good friend nearby who knows how to perform the "Heimlich Maneuver" they are lucky. If not - goodbye Charlie!

5. "<u>He rubs me the wrong way</u>". Some people enjoy having a massage, but if a competent person does not administer correct procedures, the experience can be unsatisfactory or worse it can be injurious, or it is possible to still have lumps of fat in the wrong places.

6. "<u>Sadder but wiser</u>". This refers to beer that is flat, warm and tasteless.

7. "<u>A penny for your thoughts</u>". Can you imagine if Steve Jobs only earned one cent for his "Apple" ridiculous! Right?

8. "<u>Down in the dumps</u>". Usually archaeologists spend their time doing just that and never know what goodies they will discover from ancient civilizations. Unfortunately they also get very dirty and find it difficult to climb out of the deep holes.

9. "<u>It's on the tip of my tongue</u>". I looked and looked. I really investigated thoroughly but couldn't find anything strange on my tongue tip - so I simply stuck it way out as if to say "So There!"

10. "<u>He's too big for his britches</u>". A person who is really getting fat! Or else he is buying the wrong size pants because they are on sale. Cheap! Cheap!

11. "Beauty is in the eyes of the beholder" which is why so many pretty girls marry ugly men (the guys are rich!)

12. "Get off your high horse". You can't. This is because you got older and shrunk!

13. "A man after my own heart". This guy is really a cheap skate. He needs a transplant but would rather not pay for one so he wants mine for free!

14. "It'll all come out in the wash". Trust me - It won't. I know because I tried everything from Shout to Oxi-Clean.

15. "The light at the end of the tunnel". Right now that is what I think I see, so I am signing off.

COMMON EXPRESSIONS

I'm sure you are all familiar with the expression "he let his imagination run away with him".

Now don't you think this is really silly? It almost interprets that sentence as meaning that a person is eloping with his "imagination" which actually isn't a physical being so that whole idea is ridiculous.

Indeed there are many other such expressions that are equally foolish. Take the wording "it's raining cats and dogs". Of all the dumb things that surely "takes the cake". Never in my life did I ever see a dog or a cat pelting down from the sky.

I absolutely don't think it's possible unless of course if the dog is a "Pome<u>rain</u>ian".

And how about "I gave him a piece of my mind". I don't think this makes sense either. I've never heard of this type of brain surgery. It simply hasn't been invented yet.

Then there is "I wouldn't know him from Adam". Can you imagine Eve saying this and to whom would she say it? Besides I would really think she'd know that Adam was probably the only one present without clothes, if indeed there was even another male nearby.

Finally the expression "how do you like them apples? That is the worst use of poor grammar. Even first graders would know that it should be those apples.

"My honest opinion" is that people in general should be more careful when choosing their words especially if a person like me "calls them to account".

P.S. The only almost exception I can think of is "well I'll be a monkey's uncle".

In this case the possibility is that a monkey or his gorilla relatives might have been my uncle! or if I were masculine maybe I could really be a monkey's uncle. Ha ha!

CONFUSED

I'm so confused - I think I'm out of this world and I don't mean in a complimentary way.

I really don't fit into today's technological mystique. I don't know anything about hash tags and scanners and all that stuff all the dumb people are so smart about.

Besides I understand that they get free "apps" which makes them so savvy - I, sad to say do not have any free apps and therefore I can't do anything on my emergency telephone except dial an emergency - And! right now I have an emergency! I have to get smarter! Help me somebody!

CUT IT OUT

Everything is becoming very difficult in America at the present time. The government now tells us we may have to cut back on many of the things we used to love and will hate to forfeit.

Nevertheless we should be fairly used to many of these cutbacks already because for a long time we've been doing it.

For instance we've been curtailing some of the <u>letters</u> in our wordage and the following are some of the substitutions.

Remember when we used to visit our doctors and dentists? Well now we go to our MD's and DDS's and when we receive nice invitations we promptly RSVP. Also we immediately obey our employers when they want something P.D.Q.

Our cars can have G.P.S's. Our computers have websites like AOL and, GOV, and we still avidly watch our TV's.

Kiddies of course still have to learn their ABC's if they want to graduate college with a P.H.D.

Now though we can no longer use the "N" word, and also by using the "F" word in conversations, everyone knows what you really mean, so it is definitely not O.K. to do <u>that</u>.

Then again some people frequently say "what the H" and I personally live in New York where I have to mind my "P's and Q's. New York is also the place where you can take the BMT to get to where you want to go ASAP, but you cannot "J" walk for fear of getting a ticket.

There are also many little kiddies whose mothers try to make sure they have daily BM's, and we all have our favorite TV channels like NBC, ABC, CNN, CBS, ETC.

And generally speaking a lot of people hate the T party and as time progresses I'm sure there will be a lot more "just letter" words than there were "initially" (Ha Ha Pun!).

As an aside, believe it or not, we are not the first people to resort to these "letter" type words. Even Sherlock Holmes used to say "LMN tree my dear Watson" way back in the olden days.

DATE BOOK

MONDAY
Go in
Look around
Not much there
Go out

NEXT DAY
Same thing
Go in
Look, see
Nothing nice
Leave

WEDNESDAY
Again
Same place
Nada
Boring
Go away
Sad

LATER
New place
Enter
Pretty stuff
Lots
Leave
Happy

DISEASE

I have noticed a very strange situation since I've come home from Florida. Many people I know seem to have developed wrinkles on their faces over the winter. Everywhere I look I see wrinkled people.

These people seemed perfectly okay when I left in November but now what a difference! I believe it must be a disease, and I think it is contagious because when I looked in the mirror this morning I realized I seemed to have them too!

DOES THIS GIVE YOU THE WILLIES?

Once upon a time there were 3 young girls who were extremely good friends. Their names were Bea, Zee and Kaye and were known as the alphabet pals.

Strangely they all married young men from M.I.T. Bea married Tee, Zee married Lee and Kaye married Jay.

The 3 couples remained good buddies and finally all of them had children at more or less the same time.

Zee had twin girls, Molly and Polly, Bee had two boys, Jerry and Perry and then she had a girl named Sherrie.

A few years later Kaye had the last of the group's babies. She had three boys one after the other. Barry, Harry, and Larry and unexpectedly she then had another boy she called Gary.

Pretty soon all these kiddies became old enough to attend college so the alphabet pals who now lived in different towns arranged to meet once a month to keep their friendships alive.

Bea lived on Long Island, New York. Kaye lived in Short Hills, New Jersey and Zee lived in Round Hill, Connecticut and on each New Year's Eve they usually met on Times Square to witness the count down.

One year they were fortunate enough to meet a new friend. Her name was Millie and her husband was Philly and their sons were Billy and Willie.

Isn't that silly!?

DOUBLE TROUBLE

I think I'm in trouble – terrible trouble.

BECAUSE

In my last book I wrote two articles which I personally deemed to be amusing, but could possibly be interpreted as referring to my children in a derogatory fashion. Now I must admit they were not necessarily truthful articles, but to my way of thinking they were written to convey a chuckle or two, besides I am prone to embellish a bit.

Sadly I did not know that my children would be affronted and would vocally denounce me as being a mean and unfeeling mother.

Most people who know me realize that I'm just a person who occasionally has weird and quirky thoughts, but would not intentionally demean my children, whom I truly love dearly.

In fact I do not know of any mother whose children are as generous, kind and caring as mine are.

So to Nancy, Jeff, Barbi and Kenny, please forgive me if I hurt your feelings at all. It's just that I enjoy thinking things in a funny way.

EMBARASSING MOMENTS

There is nothing more embarrassing than to be caught being insufficiently able to perform a fairly simple task, such as completing The New York Times crossword puzzles beyond Tuesdays.

Now Will Shortz (the guy who invented the puzzles) is probably a very nice person, and no doubt he tries hard to put together puzzles, suitable for all members of the general public. However I don't believe he takes into consideration the fact that, as time goes by, there is an older generation who no longer recalls "everything".

Therefore, when incompleted or incorrectly answered queries in his puzzles are penned in by this group beyond all Tuesdays, it is a situation that is to be expected, due to the memory problems of these older people. (Frankly though, many of these questions are too difficult for younger persons as well).

The worst part of this situation is when the incomplete puzzle sections of the newspaper is disposed of and put in the incinerator rooms used by the entire group of residents on the various floors of their apartment houses.

Then everybody in those buildings (who are nosy enough to read them (will be able to determine which neighbor didn't finish his or her puzzle correctly from Wednesdays through Sundays. For shame! For Shame!

EVERYONE ELSE LOVED THE MOVIE BUT I WAS BORED

I guess I'm not a very good judge of what fine entertainment is like. I say this because I recently attended a motion picture which had received wonderful accolades from "those in the know" and even from those who think they know. But I on the other hand was totally bored while viewing this film.

First of all I couldn't understand the foreign accents of the actors and I couldn't hear their voices very clearly either. ("Okay maybe I need hearing aids"). But besides all that I found the action to be forced and ineffective, and the cast seemed to be completely unable to convey anything convincing as to the story line.

Also I had to sit behind a bushy headed individual who constantly rotated his head so I really was unable to see well.

In addition, the crying baby behind me was a deterrent to my enjoyment plus the fact that my ticket cost $10 which was a further annoyance. I suppose I will be much better off in the future just watching returns on TV.

EYE SEE!

I have a big problem and I don't know what to do. The trouble is I feel boxed in. I don't see anything special out of my windows.

I am well aware that Sarah Palin can see Russia from her windows but I can't even see New Jersey from mine.

I guess I could use new glasses, maybe that would be helpful. The last eye exam I had was 3 years ago and at that time it was not suggested that I wear glasses so I have purchased "readers" since then and all seemed fine.

Now however, my "readers" (I don't mean the people who read this article) don't reflect anything-nada! However when I am in the street all seems well and then I see everything. So maybe I am only unable to see well when I'm up high - after all I do live on the 23rd floor.

Nevertheless when I am at home I am very upset when I look outside and I can't even see if it is cloudy or sunny. Oh well, I guess I'm getting older.

P.S. I just had my windows washed and I'm cured!

FEAR OF HEIGHTS

Many years ago, at age 12 to be exact, I was boarding a subway train at the station and inadvertently slipped onto the tracks. I hardly remembered the incident itself but do recall my mother saying that she lifted me up from the tracks with one hand (I doubt this but I do believe there was a general hubbub at the time and unfortunately since there was also a train in the station as well, the fear of the third rail was a factor).

Immediately afterwards though I was ushered into the office of the station manager and placed upon a rickety chair which then tilted backwards causing me to fall flat on the floor, what a situation!!

At any rate medical opinions proved that I only suffered various contusions, abrasions and hematomas which lasted for a goodly length of time, although in addition the ultimate black and blue marks were lingering reminders of my fall.

Finally of course I healed but since that time I was always reticent about heights.

Walking over gratings on the sidewalks for me was a no no and ascending or descending stairs with spaces between the steps always gave me a lurching feeling.

Also in later years when my husband used to buy opening night opera seats which were in the front row of the balcony I could not look down with ease. My stomach always had a wrenching experience and I really did not enjoy the operas at that time.

Then too while visiting the Dead Sea in Israel and looking down from above was a total disaster.

However I am lucky to be able to be in an airplane and look down below without feeling squeamish. Perhaps looking down from higher distances make me more comfortable.

I'm trying very hard to overcome this situation and now I even force myself to walk over sidewalk gratings, although I must admit I've never been in the subway since age 12. Thank god for taxis!

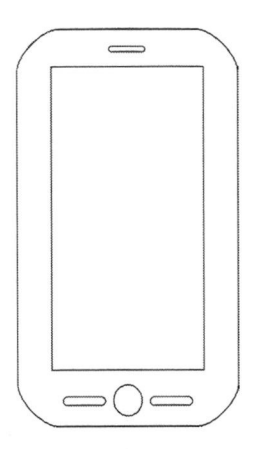

FLASH!

For those of you who may be interested, I have great news! I am now an authentic member of the "Instagram" site on my IPad.

Now I must tell you that when I started to use the. "Instagram" website, it opened up an entirely new technological world for me.

First of all I seem to know most of the people I apparently am able to follow. (I found out that this means I can contact them). You see they are mostly my grandchildren and their close friends! Since I know these "friends" fairly well, I feel very comfortable contacting them also.

Of course I am probably the oldest person on Instagram which is why several of these contacts call me insta-gram and all of them find it to be quite peculiar that I have invaded their private conversational territory.

This doesn't bother me at all as I'm happy to be included in their "doings". Although frankly, I do not always understand their wordage. It is mostly very brief, not particularly intellectual, and generally speaking it is simply a description of their daily activities, which includes shopping, theatre visits, and who met whom, where, when, and why.

But since my life does not in any measure relate to theirs they seem to find it quite hilarious that I have joined their ranks, a fact which I mentioned previously.

They comment to each other about me in wonder and have yet to comprehend my reasons for coming aboard.

Actually I did it in order to keep in touch with these little darlings because their life styles usually are too occupied with their minutia and trivialities to be bothered with me and my activities.

Consequently in order for me to become part of their lives, and to hopefully have them remember me when I am long gone, this is the only way I can burrow into their daily doings.

So now that I've joined them I discovered that they thoroughly enjoy making snide remarks about me, which they seem to do at an alarming rate.

Therefore in a retaliatory measure I am now boning up on my ability to respond effectively to these comments and - I believe I am succeeding! If you don't think so, "insta" me and read what I have to say.

FOOD FOR THOUGHT?

I have an addiction – <u>no</u> not to food stuff or any kinky sex stuff. My addiction is to the continuous re-watching of TV detective series such as "Murder She Wrote" and "Ben Matlock".

I watch them even though they are very old and replayed time after time, and I practically know the entire scripts of each episode which is played daily on high number TV channels.

This fixation of mine is probably because I am also a lover of mystery books. I try to solve the murders in each of the books I read and actually am very astute in identifying the murderous culprit in most of the volumes.

Usually it is the least likely personality who is guilty. No longer did the butler do it as that only used to be the case in bygone days.

Today's readers are more sophisticated and therefore it is not until the very last page of each volume that the killer is identified, and of course this holds true in most new TV mysteries as well.

And so far as these old TV programs are concerned, the reason I am addicted to them is, because as I mentioned before, I watch the same ones all the time, and definitely know "who done it" so I have the advantage of solving the end of each episode way before its conclusion. Then it is possible for me to switch to another TV program.

Isn't that smart of me?

HAIR TODAY GONE TOMORROW

Dear Chucky Todd
You're sure looking weird
Ever <u>since</u> you stopped shaving
And grew that new beard

But it's not that I think
You're now looking scary
<u>In fact</u> - in reverse
You just look too hairy!

HALLOWEEN AT THE HOME

A person should never underestimate their children's ability to do two things at once, and I would certainly not think of doing so with mine, or at least not with one of them namely my son Kenny.

My explanation of the above is that last evening while I was sitting quietly in my favorite chair with a pen and yellow pad in hand, trying to think of a possible subject upon which to write, my son called me from the street.

He usually does this as he thinks I enjoy listening to police or ambulance sirens and traffic noises while he is talking to me, and also so he can window shop and speak to his mother (me) simultaneously. In addition he enjoys these dual activities because "why waste time" is his motto.

At any rate during our conversation he mentioned that there was a great deal of commotion in front of the building he was passing. It seems that the tenants therein were readying themselves for their Halloween activities, which at this writing will take place tomorrow (October 31).

These people were displaying the costumes they intended wearing to each other, and were obviously having a riotously fine time discussing their expectations of a wild and exciting Halloween celebration.

This led Kenny to inquire as to what were my Halloween plans. I confessed that because of the increased aging of my neighbors, they were probably not going to be passing out candy, but most likely would simply be "passing out". I went on to further announce that most of them were coming "just as you are" - in other words "old and decrepit".

I realize that this was mean of me to say, but of course I included myself in this neighborly group so it was excusable.

To further explain the Halloween holiday, it is not generally pleasurable. The worst kind of people are cavorting in the streets, ghosts, witches, ugly old hags and many other grotesque, costumed apparitions, therefore I do not anticipate seeing any attractive people in my area.

As far as my own holiday plans are concerned I probably will spend most of the evening in a solitary manner. And when I finally do go to bed and am attired in my long white nightgown, completely devoid of facial makeup, I will then look in the mirror and see my real Halloween self - the scary looking ghost that is me! Boo!

HAPPY BIRTHDAY TO FAR AWAY DEBBERINO

DEBBIE - a girl very <u>sweet</u>
<u>Always</u> has very cold <u>feet</u>
Though she moved to "<u>Chicago</u>"
She'd prefer "<u>Marilago</u>"
Where her toes could enjoy daily <u>heat</u>

But alas Illinois is her <u>home</u>
(Which at least is warmer than "<u>Nome</u>"
Plus her family is happy
So her life there's not <u>crappy</u>
Thus I <u>doubt</u> from there she will roam!

But since she's now <u>far</u> away
And today is <u>her natal</u> day
We <u>wrote</u> her this <u>ditty</u>
And tried <u>hard</u> to be witty
So <u>Deb</u> - what more can we<u> say!</u>

All the best -luv Bernicerino

HARKEN

For those of you with I.B.S.
Or allergic to items lactic
I would suggest a diet change
To be a healthy tactic

NEWS ITEM

Nelson Mandela
A wonderful fella
Too bad you left us so soon
So sad it is clear
That you left our sphere
And now reside near the moon

DIETARY ADVICE

If no butter, cheese, nor milk
Should cross your lips
This abstinence might help to slim your hips
So heed my words - avoid the foods above
Just eat more fruit and veggies
That you'll soon grow to love

HELLO

"Hello everybody, I want to introduce myself". "I'm a page in a book". "Actually I'm not just any page", I'm probably the most important one"

"No I'm not the first page or the last page". However I'm sort of in the last part of the final chapter of the book".

This is where you can probably find out who killed the guy or the girl, or maybe who was shacking up with whom, or when the guy asks the girl to marry him, or even when the girl finds out that she's adopted and that her neighbor down the street is her birthmother.

In any event I'm very valuable, I'm actually what sells the most volumes particularly if I have very vulgar words written on me.

Today of course most people know that books are not selling well because of all the nooks and kindles, etc, so therefore a solitary page like me is not worth much monetarily. Nevertheless I'd like to think that I have importance way beyond mere cash.

Therefore I would appreciate it if when you next pick up a book that you do not skip my place in the volume.

In other words absolutely do not peek when you get to the end of the volume before you get to my spot.

Thank you

<small>THIS BOOK MAY BE MY LASTER AND ALSO MY WORSTER WHICH IS BADDERA THAN AWFULER</small>

HEY HEY DOC

As mentioned recently in an article a few pages back, I went to my doctor because I had lost my voice.

So after my examination I was ushered into his office where he entered my current medical data onto my chart.

He then <u>vocally</u> recorded my condition while he was writing about it, and announced that it was "acute virus". I was quite surprised because I didn't think it was so adorable.

HI JESUS!

I just heard an interview with Bill O'Reilly who has recently written a book about Jesus the Man.

He told his audience that he was influenced by the Holy Spirit when he wrote this book and when he was questioned about this statement he explained it in this manner.

He said that he himself was an ardent Catholic and a firm believer in the bible as being entirely truthful.

So when he said he felt that the Holy Spirit came to him in the middle of the night to tell him to write this book, he thought it was because of his religious <u>belief</u>, not because he actually felt Jesus's presence when he got the idea. On the other hand he did not think he would have thought of writing it unless Jesus did put the idea in his head.

So much for the explanations of holy visitation.

(P.S. I get my own ideas!)

HOME IS WHERE YOU HAVE TO PAY RENT

I live in a "<u>com</u>plex" which can sometimes be very complex, well, not actually com<u>plex</u>. Just a little unusual at times.

You see it houses many people from different former residences and life styles. They (these people) are all extremely unlike. Some are nice, some not so nice and some in between. So a new person living here has to try to fit in, which takes time.

Now occasionally a new resident can accidentally and fortunately meet a very nice person and think wow! We're going to be good friends, then the very next week when he or she is in the mail room picking up the daily mail, which usually consists of the many envelopes that are stuffed with requests for donations to organizations he never heard of, he or she suddenly notices a sign on the wall announcing the demise of that "new friend", the one they really liked. This is really a sad moment (Now they have to find a new BFF).

So off they go to their apartment to brood sadly for awhile. Then they perk up and decide to go to the so called fancy restaurant in the arcade.

After perusing the list of "today's specials" they settle for soup and a baked apple. Very tasty they think! This is truly a great place!

And after this nice little repast these new residents venture back to the arcade where a wheeled group of people exist. There they are - almost an army - A myriad amount of people (not so young) sporting their wheels. Some of them are sitting in little cars and zigzagging in and out of other people's traffic lanes, where baskety types of vehicles try to avoid an oncoming collision. There are also triangular three wheelers, and some aide chauffeured wheelchairs are present as well.

Therefore it is very evident that I live on a race track. There is so much mobility here that it is almost impossible to avoid the heavy traffic. Pretty soon I believe all the residents will need driver's licenses just to go to the drugstore in the middle of this arcade.

That drugstore by the way is really an O.T.B. Almost everybody who enters bets on everything. All over the walls are signs notifying prospective bettors how much money was won there in the previous week- Lies! All of it is lies! Big fat lies! Nobody ever <u>really</u> wins- Ever!

There are also food emporiums next to the drugstore - two of them - one fruity one and another that sells packaged and canned foods. They sometimes overlap product wise, so it's occasionally hard to know who sells what. Happily everything is good in both places.

Also a beauty parlor is situated at the very end of the space. This shop is like the League of Nations. All different countries are represented by the operators. You can have an Iranian, Russian, Spanish, Chinese, or an Israeli hairdresser do your do. But somehow your hair always looks the same.

I forgot! There are also three swimming pools and boy you should see the bodies! Esther Williams would drop dead- oops! She really is dead!

At any rate when all is said and done I'm thoroughly enjoying my life here, so come on down and visit me.

HOPE

This is the "Hour of Reckoning". Actually in about four hours we will know whether the Republicans will achieve their goal and shut down the government. If this happens I believe our world as we know it will decidedly change, and not for the better.

Isn't it shameful that a great country like America should have such divisiveness among it's lawmakers?

Didn't our founding fathers hope to establish a peaceful, safe and thriving country with hopes that the lives of <u>all</u> its citizens would do well financially, socially and religiously?

Isn't that why the original dwellers in this part of the world came here in the first place?

They presumably hated what was happening in the part of the world from whence they came, and by coming here and suffering and working hard for so many years it was only to establish comfortable lives for their families and friends. They had high hopes that America would become a paradise for all of them.

Therefore isn't it stupid that so many of the present members of our Congress should dispute what their own relatives yearned for?

Shouldn't they be grateful for their own success and good luck, and be pleased to think that the same things should be available for all Americans?

So why don't we all come to the same conclusion and wish the best for America and its worthy citizens.

This article was written months before this book was published so hopefully what I've said above has had some impact, and a successful conclusion has been reached by the two opposing factions of our government.

HOW I CHANGED MY WORLD AND WHEN IT STARTED

I was 15 years old, at which time I set in motion the events that ultimately changed my world and the lives of all my children, grandchildren and great grandchildren.

I know that sounds amazing but no doubt unusual events have changed the lives of other people in similar circumstances.

Nevertheless this is my particular story.

Usually I went to my high school every morning with six other girls which cost 10 cents for each of us in a taxicab.

However one morning our taxi did not arrive and I was forced to ride the subway which was especially crowded. It was winter time as well so I was wearing a heavy brown winter coat with a red fox collar. As there were no available seats, I was forced to stand next to a pole and there was a young man about 17 standing there as well.

Since it was so crowded the fluff from my red fox collar kept popping into his mouth and naturally we started a conversation during my apologies to him. I found out he was a senior at Stuyvesant High School which was on the lower west side while my school was on the east side so we spoke about the various contrasts in our two schools and actually had a lovely conversation. I had to leave the train first because I had to take a shuttle train over to the east side so I said goodbye and left.

When I got home that afternoon I related the amusing story about my fur collar and the young man. My sister who was much older asked me, "did you make a date with him"? I, who never had a date in my life was shocked into replying, "of course not" and promptly forgot the entire incident.

However the next morning when I was again forced to take the subway to school, the young man whose name I ultimately discovered was Barney was waiting for me on the station. He said "you left so quickly that I didn't get your telephone number".

To make a long story short, I made a date with Barney which set in motion all the following incidents.

We became very good friends and my family practically adopted him. As he had no father and his mother was a busy newspaper journalist who was rarely at home he therefore led a lonesome personal life.

There were times, when I finally did start dating about my 16th year, and Barney would spend the evening with my parents while I was out with a date. I think he really considered them to be his auxiliary parents and I was like the sister he never had.

At any rate when his mother passed away he decided to move to Chicago where he really knew no one. Since I had a little friend Elaine who had moved to Chicago (before I knew Barney), I suggested that he call her as I figured this way he could make a friend who had mutual ties to his New York life (meaning me).

P.S. They did end up becoming friends and actually got married. A few years later when they had a baby I was named as the baby's godmother and was invited to Chicago to see the little one.

By the way in those days travel was mostly by railroad and it was unusual for a young girl (me) to go alone to a strange city. Nevertheless I finally did so and this is what happened next. A few weeks before I was to leave on my trip, at a family wedding I met an older cousin of mine who had married a young man in Peoria Illinois. I told her that I was going to Chicago in a few weeks and she was so excited to think that a relative of hers would be so near her new home. She then insisted that I visit her while I was in Chicago which was so close to Peoria, plus she said I'd have a wonderful time there.

I of course, was not adventurous in those years, nevertheless I convinced my parents to let me extend my trip to visit my cousin Lee and luckily I got their consent. Therefore I set out on my adventure and spent a few days in Chicago visiting Barney, Elaine and their adorable baby boy and then took the Rocket train to Peoria where I expected to stay for about 10 days and get to know something about the Midwest, as I was such an innocent New Yorker, and eager to learn about the rest of the country.

When I arrived, the first thing Lee did was have the local newspaper send someone to her home to take my picture, which was placed on a full page under the heading "visiting cousin in Peoria". I was famous! This would never have happened in New York and I was truly impressed.

Then she informed me that I had been invited to several luncheons where I received gifts and also a few young men called me for dates. This last I did not understand at all and told Lee that I didn't want any young man to spend money on a stranger they would never see again, so I refused to go out with any of them. But then she insisted that "they will think something is wrong with you if you don't accept these dates". So to avoid offending her I consented to abide by the Midwestern custom and date a few people, one of whom I ultimately married -Albert Zakin

I must say I loved living in Peoria. I loved the Midwesterners and of course I loved Al and our ultimate lives together.

However the second world war circumstances then forced us to move to Fort Worth, Texas where our daughter Nancy was born and then two years later we made our final move back to New York.

Several years after that we bought a house in Lawrence, Long Island right next door to the Rothensteins whose parents we had met while we were living in Palm Beach, Florida. They became our very dear friends through the years and one day Eddie Rothenstein's cousin visited them and saw Nancy in the backyard. She asked if Nancy would be willing to date a nice young man she knew. Nancy said she would. So the date was arranged and Nancy spent a very nice evening with him. Unfortunately he was really too short for her but asked her if she would like to date his roommate, as he thought they would get along well. Again Nancy agreed to this and started dating Mark Stern who was very nice looking, smart and a lawyer with a most prestigious law firm. However Al and I were always skeptical about him and were not convinced that he was the right choice for Nancy.

Nevertheless they did marry and had two wonderful little children, Andy and Lizzie.

Things seemed to be fine until the day some eight years later when Mark told Nancy that he was gay, which we always suspected, and had a boyfriend. Wow! This was before men came out of the closet and we all were shocked but happy that he revealed his situation.

Divorce of course was inevitable and luckily it was very amicable.

Then one day about six months later, Carol Weiss, a girl we didn't know but who was a member of our mutual golf club (The Woodmere Club) saw Nancy at the pool and knowing the unusual (at that time) story about her imminent divorce proceedings, she asked her if she would care to meet a very nice man with whom her husband worked.

Nancy said yes and met Jeff. To this day we have to thank Carol for this wonderful gesture she made to Nancy. Jeff and Nancy have been married for 32 years and their 5 wonderful children have blended and love one another as if they were of the same blood. It is truly a miracle tale.

Ultimately all five (3 of them were Jeff's children) are now happily married and have children of their own. Lizzie is the only one to be divorced and amicably so. Jeff, her former husband was introduced to his present wife by of all people, Lizzie's brother Andy and Lizzie is now very happily married to Jon Tisch whose grandmother I knew years ago, so it all comes back to my brown coat with the fox collar. If it hadn't been for the taxicab being unable to take me to high school that day way back then, none of these scenarios would have taken place. Isn't fate a remarkable thing?

So now you know how I changed my world.

HOW TO BE A GOOD "SKATE"

During my high school years at Julia Richman on 68th Street and 2nd, I spent a good amount of time roller skating home through Central Park on to 86th Street and Riverside drive, where I lived.

In those days roller skates had 4 wheels and I was particularly adept at maneuvering the pair I owned.

Generally, if it was a Thursday, I would stop off on Central Park West where I'd go to the Museum of Natural History. In that wondrous building they had a marvelous candy store, where on Thursdays it was fully stocked with huge bars of toffee conveniently priced for high school students at 5 cents a bar.

Naturally because I was addicted to those bars, I was a frequent customer at the store!

However just before I got to the museum I had to finish chewing on my pickle which I usually purchased out of a barrel in a store next to Don Q's drug store across the street from Julia Richman.

At that time I was an excellent purchaser of junk food. I really had a sense of its good quality plus the fact that I had an insatiable appetite and besides I had a very skinny frame so I could easily accommodate any number of items that were not to be found in my mother's grocery closet or refrigerator (pardon me- I mean ice box).

At any rate after I arrived on 86th Street and Broadway, my final stop was at Tip Toe Inn's Bakery which was very famous and where I would buy a jelly doughnut. Then of course I could skate directly home where my mother would kindly offer me a glass of milk and a social tea biscuit.

But oh how I really miss those stops that I made before I ultimately arrived at my apartment house.

"Those were the days" as they say.

HOW TO BE THE TEACHER OF THIS CLASS?

There is a lady who lives several steps from the ocean in Palm Beach, in a circular apartment house, which is white as the snow that presently shrouds many unfortunate cities in the Eastern part of the United States.

This lady usually holds court in a room at one end of this apartment house, where on most Tuesday afternoons in the winter months, several ladies including me convene as a class, and enjoy dripping words out of their pens onto various hunks of paper.

These words are meant to ingratiate, appeal to, and impress the lady, who is in charge. (i.e. the teacher).

Now to officiate as "that special one", the teacher usually tries to appear official. She generally is attired in attractive clothing, sits at the head of the writing table with a funny looking device which prints words, and then she issues writing suggestions to her entrapped group of would be wordsmiths.

Sadly these ladies have recently had their numbers depleted due to ailments, other occupations, and possibly a scarcity of paper.

Nevertheless the remaining faithfuls dutifully complete their assignments and then orally relate them to the group.

Laughter from this body of folks is encouraged, criticism is accepted with good grace, and the teacher generally blithely ignores any obvious literacy faux pas. Incidentally this teacher exacts no payment from the class.

To sum it up, to be a teacher who can meet the standards of snooty Palm Beach, requires someone who can administer kindly critical judgment, be able to praise if possible, and to be an extremely lovable human being. Guess who meets this criteria?

HOW TO LINK OUT

I have to admit that I am very gullible and I believe almost everything I am told by supposedly honest and upright people.

I would never expect any of my family or close friends to deliberately try to entice me into doing anything that I would morally consider to be against my better judgment.

However I recently and inadvertently became a part of a fairly new website called "LinkedIn". It suddenly appeared on my computer screen and queried if I knew any of the several people whose names and pictures were mentioned.

Being truthful as well as gullible (as I wrote above), I dutifully checked the pictured names which were indeed some of my friends and family members. Little did I know that by doing so, I had been hooked into the "LinkedIn" group which is essentially a business site.

These same people want to know with whom I am presently linked businesswise, and would I please communicate with them as quickly as possible.

Therefore I am wondering if I should do so as I'm actually retired, thus my current business (none) is <u>none</u> of their business anyway.

Nevertheless since they are good friends and include some family members as well, I am loath to irritate them.

So do I pretend to be the CEO of nothing? Or maybe a major stockholder in my refrigerator? It so happens that I am a verified Vice President of my clothes closet, where I oversee all my belongings on a daily basis. This position can some day lead to the Presidency of said closet, once I purchase more stock (sweaters, pants, tops, etc).

And by the way I am also the sole owner of a fairly large corporation (although it only exists in the middle of my body).

At any rate, I am now in a puzzled state as to how I should proceed with this "LinkedIn" website.

At the moment I believe my only other option (I don't mean Wall Street options) is to delete all its messages.

HOW TO VOTE

Election Day is finally here and all we have to do is place an X next to any names we choose. We don't even have to know or like the person - we just have to vote, which is the patriotic thing to do.

Of course we've probably all had telephone calls lately (or I should say recordings) from candidates applying for positions in our area that require replacement persons.

However the real person never calls us - just their recordings which generally sounds as if he or she is our best friend. Our first name is always used and this person pledges complete devotion to all the popular causes being espoused, and sincerely makes promises galore for everything we desire in a candidate.

Naturally once the election takes place, most of these promises are forgotten and these people never call us again (except for money). Besides we usually forget their names anyway.

Nevertheless politics being what it is (a dishonest, dishonorable and deceitful form of governing our country, states and cities), we have to accept it for what it is and simply hope for the best.

So next time you go into the voting booth, remember it really doesn't matter how you vote as you probably are going to elect a terrible person anyway.

IDEAS IN THE NIGHT

What is a poem?
It's thought and word

What is life?
It's pulse and blood

What's is religion?
It's god and prayer

What is love?
It's kiss and caress

What is the sky?
It's air and bird

What is earth?
It's grass and mud

What is alone?
It's no one there

And what is fear?
Despair and stress

IF AND WHERE TO SNACK

Snacking! To my mind this is truly an activity worth developing. I believe it is practically an art form, although not museum worthy.

In fact for some people daily snacking is the most important segment of their 24 hour everyday routine and is quite popular in every country, but especially in the U.S.A.

This particular habit can take place at any time of the day or night, and most people snack frequently. It is definitely not a casual every so often indulgence.

A person can start sneaking a snack shortly after breakfast, maybe even before lunch, 2 hours after lunch, prior to dinner, and certainly before going to bed.

Ordinarily snacks can consist of any variety of items. But potato chips, candy, pickles, ice cream, nuts and various other "can't resist" types of edibles are the usual. However one can easily find odd things to ingest as well.

Also these things do not necessarily have to be purchased all at once, so long as at least a few of them (even leftovers) are always on hand if need be, and it is a known fact that nobody of any consequence would ever dare to be caught sans a detectable item to consume when their tummys indicate that snack time has arrived.

But! au contraire many ordinary people belie the fact that they <u>do</u> snack. It is often <u>not</u> considered to be a commendable act. In fact, generally speaking it is a hidden embarrassment, albeit a delightful occupation.

On the other hand little children are allowed to have snacks openly. In fact specific times are set aside in most schools for just such food intakes. Nevertheless adults are denied such a privilege.

And if you are with a group of close friends, they will generally never reveal that they are snackers, but if you probe them a bit then "the truth will out".

Now I personally do not "snack". What I do is openly raid my refrigerator or grocery closet and declare to myself that my extra meal time has arrived.

In that way it is my opinion that what I do is nobody's business and just a way to satisfy my enticing food longings.

By the way, as a general observation I have noticed that most snackers either already are or <u>become fat!</u>

(Me too!)

ILL ANNOYING

So here I am nursing a cold -well not exactly "nursing" a cold because that would imply that I was lactating and feeding this thing, which I am not doing because I actually hate it. So I certainly would not feed it intentionally just to keep it alive. As a matter of fact I would really rather kill it before it destroys me.

It's not even my cold. It belongs to someone in Chicago where I spent last weekend, both willingly and pleasurably, until I arrived home with this unforeseen and unwelcome ailment.

I have a suspicion that some Midwesterner foisted it on me when I wasn't looking. Could it have been that Russian taxi driver with the Jewish accent? Or the sales person at See's Candy store? I'm sure it was one of them - that driver did not seem to be trustworthy so most likely it was him.

On the other hand it could have been the waiter at the Pump Room. I was having such a good time there and really enjoyed the great dinner, but I do recall hearing the waiter sneeze while he was serving my soup. So who knows?

At any rate I am not going to treat this thing as if it were really mine. I know my rights and I won't be subjected to any out of state illness! So there!

P.S. Back in New York and subsequent reactions to my cold:

Saturday
1. My daughter Nancy - feel better soon
2. My daughter-in-law Barbie - oh my god!
3. Patsy - do you want me to come or are you going to the beauty parlor?
4. Bea Diamond - don't come to play bridge, I'll bring my own cards
5. Ceil Berman - It takes 10 days.
6. Barbie again - do you want me to call Patsy - who's going to fix your soup - oh my god!
7. Ceil Berman - again - it takes 10 days

Sunday
1. Nancy - you sound better
2. Patsy - looking forward to seeing someone in 23D
3. Barbie - you feel better? Thank god!
4. Ceil Berman - it takes 10 days
5. Bea Diamond - how are you - you sound worse

Monday
1. Nancy - how are you - you sound better
2. Barbie - didn't call
3. Ceil Berman - you sound better - it didn't take so many days after all
4. Patsy - you look better - do you want some soup?

Tuesday
1. Cecil Berman - you sounded better yesterday. I told you it takes 10 days.
2. Nancy - I think you're better
3. Patsy - you look better
4. Me - I think I'm better :-)

IL PLEUT

Good morning everybody. No! Scratch that. It is <u>not</u> a good morning. It is a <u>terrible</u> morning and it is Florida. Yes! Florida that southern state where the natives promise to deliver beautiful sunny climes and balmy, soft, lovely breezes <u>all</u> the time especially for northern visitors to enjoy.

Ha! I do mean ha! Because I am presently in that sunny place for the winter, in the town of Palm beach which is considered to be the queen of luxury in that state.

But instead of the divine weather from which I anticipated deriving pleasure, it is now pouring. Yes the drops are constantly flooding the entire area of Palm Beach County with rain, rain, rain, and more rain, plus wind and cold freezing weather all over the town!

Luckily I am indoors but I absolutely am fearful of leaving my cocoon. as I had wonderful plans for this day all to no avail. I am now stuck within the confines of my apartment with nothing to do except listen to my TV, read, make telephone calls to dry people in other states, and eat, snack, ingest food, swallow, devour and feast.

Thank heavens I have many tasty items in my cupboards and refrigerator so I can indulge myself food wise during this deluge, providing of course that it doesn't last more than a week.

So, if any of you readers are smart you will take heed of this warning. "Do not attempt a southern trip in the near future. Remember umbrellas can turn inside out, raincoats are not flattering and shoes can get permanently soaked and become unwearable forever".

Go to Arizona – the winter weather there is terrific.

INSOMNIA

The other night I was extremely tired so I went to bed early. <u>Really early</u> and was happily very sound asleep for 2 hours but then everything changed in my sleeping pattern.

This was because a good friend, who has a habit of staying up late, called me on her cell phone with some kind of odd message (presumably important to her) and from that time on I was wide awake and absolutely could not return to slumber land.

I twisted and punched my two pillows to no avail. Then I tried getting up and drinking a glass of water, then I tried punching my pillows again, then I got up to go to the bathroom, then I punched the pillows again, then I turned on the air conditioner, then I read a few pages in a nearby book, then I punched the pillows again. Then I turned off the air conditioner, and then I thought of punching my friend!

And then it was morning and time to get up!

I THINK I AM LISTLESS

What should I do? I don't remember everything as well as I used to.

For instance if I'm going on a trip I have to make a list of everything I will need on said trip.

But then I forget where I put the list, so then I have to make another list, and then I find the first list and have to throw away the second list, but then I realize I have forgotten to put some of the things that were on that second list back on the first list, and I'm left with the first original list when most likely if I was actually going on the trip, the second list would have been better than the first list, which I will never use anyway, since I'm not going on that trip.

Therefore the entire list making becomes a waste of time and besides I don't think I'll ever remember to put everything on any list if I ever go on another trip which is doubtful,

I'VE GOT YOU UNDER MY SKIN

At this writing it is mid August and I am infested with teensy, wee little flies.

Even if I am sitting quietly – perhaps reading or listening to the TV, these pesky little fellows fly around and light upon my person. They are so small that I can't catch them. I would very much like to annihilate them, but no matter how fast I swat they are even faster and so far I've not been able to commit very many murders.

The worst of this situation is that they really think they live here, but they don't pay rent, and so far I've been supplying them with food. – ME!

Since I am not here in the winter I can not be sure if they are year round inhabitants, nevertheless even their part time residence is not welcome, and I would appreciate their immediate departure.

They are driving me absolutely "Buggy" So what to do? Would an exterminator be able to destroy them completely? Should I move out? Do I simply wait until I am ready to leave for Florida? Or is there any other solution (I don't mean liquid) that might be possible to eliminate my anguish as well as my flies?

Oops! There goes another one! I am really beside myself (which means there are two of us)

<u>Please</u> "any person" advise me as to how I can correct my dire situation as soon as possible – preferably before October

I WONDER

Where does Anthony Wiener go from here?

Will he open a hot dog stand called Weiner's Weiner's?

Will he become just a Whiner?

Or will he give up his bad habit by becoming a Wean-er?

Or will he realize he will never be a winner?

Or change his name to Spitzer and get a divorce?

JOAN

We know that birthdays come and go
And they're happy for most <u>folks</u>
And at <u>parties</u> for these honorees
There's speeches and or jokes

But when a person we all know is celebrating hers
We <u>all</u> are at a loss for words
The day that this occurs

That's <u>because</u> she's very special
And lovely, kind and pretty
<u>Plus</u> of <u>course</u> she's full of spice
But most of all she's <u>witty</u>

And so today we only hope
That <u>she'll</u> find many joys
In celebration with her friends
Plus Laurie and her boys

Therefore we raise our glasses now
With wine or maybe coke
To wish you Happy Birthday Joan
And believe me- that's no joke!

This Book May Be My Laster And Also My Worster Which Is Baddera Than Awfuler

LATE FOR THE DATE

I hereby admit to not being so young anymore, however I certainly do have a fair amount of wits about me, and do not believe that my brain is addled nor am I a ditz, or in any way <u>completely</u> ditzy.

At any rate, I was recently invited to my daughter-in-laws birthday party which was originally to be held at a particular restaurant in New York. I was then advised that the party place was changed, and by email I was informed of the new address.

Dressed to the nines, I hired a car and driver and was driven to New York and arrived there way ahead of the time I was actually due. When we arrived at the address I was given, it proved to be the wrong place, and since I had no cell phone with me (I had such a small purse) and could not remember the cell numbers of the people involved in the party planning, there was very little hope I could grace my hosts with my presence.

Finally after much confusion, pleading and exhaustive pursuance of anyone who could help me, the proper restaurant was reached, and even though I was the very last person to arrive, I was greeted enthusiastically despite my being beyond fashionably late.

Nevertheless I particularly noticed an undercurrent and buzz in the room such as "do you think she's losing it? "After all she isn't so young", "she look's okay but wouldn't you think she'd know <u>where</u> she was going?"

I probably would have humbly accepted these nasty whispering comments as being valid, but my mental reputation was finally vindicated when I got back home after the party and consulted the email I had received with the <u>"incorrect"</u> address of the restaurant.

I firmly believe the party planner (no relation) simply made the error in my email only and so the other guests did not suffer my humiliation.

I got my revenge however, in an odd way because the menu in my daughter-in-laws honor,(and that was given to all the guests) had an equally unusual error. One of the choices listed under the entree heading was "spaghettini with spicy <u>crap</u> and meyer lemon". I did <u>not</u> order it!

LATITUDE

I have just discovered that certain words have extremely powerful and unusual connotations.

As for instance - Latitude

Now <u>Latitude</u> actually has two meanings. The first one shows that a person can give another person or thing a certain amount of leeway or freedom.

The other meaning indicates the space from the equator on a map, which denotes that the more latitude that exists is equal to the increased land area that is covered.

Therefore we can presume that if we give Mr. Putin more latitude in <u>Both</u> instances he can claim additional land as well as the freedom to obtain it.

Nationally it then appears that he's a winner no matter what. Thus proving the power of the word latitude Wow!

LONGEVITY - LONG MAY IT LIVE!

If you live long enough- you may either become very wise or very stupid. You may also relate incidents that never happened and pretend that they did.

These things are all possibilities but not necessarily so.

Certainly younger people will not be able to dispute whatever you tell them because they were not alive when these things supposedly took place.

Then too old people won't dispute them either as they probably have bad memories or none at all, therefore they have no frame of reference.

At any rate as an older person, it is entirely safe to say outrageous and untruthful things without fear of reprisal.

But young people- being young- do not have the advantage of knowing all the things we older folks take for granted. We are very familiar with everything that happened years ago that were so interesting, exciting, unusual, and even devastating at the time they took place, while the younguns only know what they <u>know</u> or think what they know <u>now</u>.

Of course the primary reason older people can relate tall tales is because it is a known fact that they (the older people) have a greater knowledge (or can make believe they have) of past events (but not present ones).

Although this too is not necessarily true as I particularly recall my son at a very young age asking me. "How was it in your day mommy"? My answer to him at the time was very evasive, I simply said "it's <u>still</u> my day "Kenny".

Luckily I am presently able to refer to my present events (within reason) as well as my past ones but I'm not sure which were better.

We'll have to see what the future is like before I pass judgment, that is if I'm able to remember!

LOST AND FOUND

I hate to admit it but I lost it. I really lost it. Actually I lost it twice. I'm not talking about my temper, my memory, my mind or any other equally valuable thing. Although I lost an exceedingly important item and I thought it was forever, but! I found it and I found it twice so isn't that great?

Most likely you want to know what that lost item was. Well, it happened to be the key to my car! I really did lose it twice.

The first time was when I had just been in a stationery store two blocks from my apartment and when I left the store and got back in my car there was no key. Not in my handbag and not on the dash board of the car. No place! So what to do? I returned to the stationery store and looked all over the floor as well as the owner's desk to no avail. Then I went back to the car, looked under it, behind it and even in the gutter. No dice, no key! I went back to the stationery store again diligently hunting around the area where I had been standing and sadly I found nothing resembling a lost key.

Naturally I then dejectedly returned to the car and decided to walk home where thankfully I had an extra key. However just before that I had a sudden urge to open the door of the car once more and again give the front seat another little poke about, when lo and behold, tucked into a corner there it was, my wonderful key! I could have leaped into the air for joy but instead I went to Publix across the street and made several unnecessary purchases to celebrate my success in finding the key.

Then I went home at last, including all my bags, with the sense of relief finding the key brought to me.

Thus the evening passed by pleasantly. The next day was an unusually lovely warm, sunny Florida special day and I decided to go back to Publix as I had actually forgotten to buy the thing I really needed, which was orange juice.

I then picked up my handbag and fished around for my newly found car key but oh no! It was an impossibility. I had misplaced it again, it really wasn't there, therefore another hunt was in order.

This time I had to go back downstairs to the car to see if I had left it in the trunk which I remembered opening but it wasn't there. Again I feverously dug into every corner of that car just as I had yesterday but again it was a fruitless search.

Dejectedly I returned to my apartment and decided to admit to the fact that I had indeed "lost it" and I didn't mean my key this time. I had to come to terms with the fact that my memory was possibly disintegrating with age. I even thought that I might have thrown away the key with one of the Publix bags and then once again miraculously a flash of light filtered into my head and joy oh joy I found my car key in the bag in which I kept my writing material, which had been in the car the day before. The moral of this tale is that at last I am once again a whole person with my memory intact and a car that can be driven, so long as the key is inserted in the dashboard.

MAIL

MAIL RECEIVED

Dear Bernice,

I don't know if that is your name but it seems to be the way you sign your books so that is what I will call you. At any rate, I think you write like a jerk!

In fact you write like a real jerk! You actually have "nothing" to say and you don't say "nothing" very well.

You must think that the average readers (and of course I'm sure all of your possible readers are no better than average) don't expect very much from you, so therefore that is what they get (not very much).

You certainly must be aware that you can't spell. Your grammar is terrible, and there is very little else I can write about you without being either abrasive or abusive.

Nevertheless I wish you the best. Sorry - I am rude.

MAILED ANSWERED

Dear rude,

Speaking of grammar - how come you don't capitalize your name?

As for my writing, it's the thought that "counts" and I'm not talking "math".

Anyway, thank you for your comments.

The Real Jerk

MASON

Mason my 10 year old great grand daughter is notably both amusing and wise beyond her years.

And so one day when I plaintively said to her-"Mason-you are really so grownup", I hardly know how old you are.

Her reply was - "Well most people think I'm a 45 year old person stuck in a 10 year old body".

And I truly believe this is true.

MAULED AT THE MALL

I have a big problem. I think I can never go to a mall especially if I emerge laden with packages containing beautiful items I might have purchased at bargain prices, because I could be shot! Yes there are evil people lurking about just waiting to pounce upon innocent customers who simply wish to reach their cars, deposit their goodies and get home safely.

In my case this could be very unfortunate as I am actually not the garden variety of a mall shopper.

I am a person who ordinarily goes to places like Bergdorfs, therefore I would not expect to be caught "dead" in a mall. But supposing I was found to be demised in one and (verily) dismissed from this life by a bullet discharged from a gun that was in the possession of a mentally deranged fiend, who chose me to be his victim. How would this situation be appraised if it were to appear in the local papers particularly in The Palm Beach Shiny Sheet, because in that case my social reputation would be ruined. People would probably whisper things like "what was she doing in a mall of all places" or "I understand she didn't appear to have her hair set recently" or even "she was carrying several packages so she actually had been shopping". Oh god what an embarrassment that would be.

Therefore people should always be careful about where they die. One never knows who might find them especially if it is in an undesirable place, and certainly a mall is the least prestigious location for anyone to be discovered in a non living condition.

Warning! If by chance a public departure from life seems to be imminent, then hopefully it will be in a dignified setting preferably Paris or Venice, or if it is in America, then Chanel or Hermes might do. If it happens at a friend›s home be sure that person lives on Park or Fifth Avenue never above 86th Street!

ME

I don't write anything for intellectuals as I am not one myself and therefore am not qualified to do so.

I don't write for sad people because I tend to see the humorous side of life.

I don't write for the very rich people because they have better things to do with their money than buy my books.

I don't write for the poor because they don't have the time or money to read my books.

I certainly don't write for the very staunch Republicans because we have different view points.

Frankly I don't think there are any people I do write for so why the heck do I keep doing it.

Maybe just for me!

ME AND THEM

I hate to admit it but I am really deeply troubled because I believe I am stuck in the wrong age group of people.

You see most of my friends; (of whom I am quite fond) have ailments, many of them. These people visit physicians on a more than regular basis, and they describe their bodily disorders to me very frequently.

They also complain constantly and agonize daily about their shoulder and back pains, stomach conditions, hip problems and ongoing dysfunctions of one thing and another. So frankly our daytime conversations have become quite limited subject wise.

Besides at night time these same folks avidly watch reruns - can you imagine? That means movies from 40 years ago - wow! Also when they say they are going shopping they are referring to the grocery store or Costco.

Now, au contraire, my children's friends are entirely different. They are in a wonderful age group -when my friends discuss having difficulties with their joints, my children's friends go to joints for pleasure, and when they go shopping they come home with boxes from Saks, and Bergdorf as well as from fancy hidden away places like "1521 Madison Ave" upstairs.

In addition my children's acquaintances all have "apps" while I personally have only one measly little app, and <u>my</u> pals have none at all.

I can tell you right now that I want more apps, I <u>need</u> more apps. My children's friends have a load of them like "cookoo birds" or "angry birds". They have so many different kinds, which enhance their lifestyles immeasurably. Therefore I am positive that "apps" are a really good thing to have - especially in "today's world".

Speaking of "today's world", my children and their pals are all very much "in it" while all my buddies have either sadly departed from "it" entirely, or are not enjoying their world at all.

As I mentioned before <u>my</u> friends watch reruns but my children's companions go to "openings"! What a difference there seems to be in the age span activities between our two generations.

Well I guess I could go on forever talking about this comparison subject, but I am presently in my dermatologist's office (not that I have anything major wrong with me) and I believe I'm his next patient. So….Adious!

MISTAKEN IDENTITY

Many years ago in the 5 towns of the South Shore, I was crossing a side street in Cedarhurst enroute to my upholsterer, when an SUV coming up the street stopped me as I attempted to cross. The driver was wearing a yamaka (the town had recently become quite orthodox Jewish) and was accompanied by his wife whose head was encased in a decidedly religious type of scarf.

He said "pardon me", do you know any store around here that sells lox? I said yes, that there was one right up the street on Central Avenue.

He further questioned me by asking "what else do they sell". I was surprised by his question but politely replied "yes they have bagels, cream cheese and other appetizing items".

At that moment he started laughing and said "you know you are very cute" and then added "I was looking for a store with "locks" for my doors as "I just moved to town".

We both got hysterical laughing and his wife said "you should send this incident into Readers Digest". I never did, however I also never forgot my new neighbor.

MY APARTMENT

There is a well known expression which says "nobody ever knows what goes on behind the closed doors of another person's home".

Well I am going to refute that statement by telling you everything about my apartment. I.E.

Very often when I'm about to enter said apartment the telephone is ringing, so I dash in and get to the nearest telephone (I have 5). This one is on top of a credenza which is against a wall of my very sizeable foyer, so I pick up the still ringing phone expecting to hear a friendly voice, instead the phone instantly stops ringing and displays a message which says "this phone is off base - try another phone".

So then I go to another still ringing phone which is in the kitchen to the left of the foyer. This kitchen has a black floor, black countertops and a black telephone, which is sitting right next to a black toaster oven.

It is also a very dark kitchen because it has no windows, therefore it is almost impossible to find the telephone.

But not to worry! I go straight ahead through the kitchen to the dining alcove -actually a very nice little room. It is bright and sunny with a land phone on a book shelf. (I have bookshelves in every room in my apartment).

I then try to pick up the still ringing phone receiver on my phone which sadly stops ringing as soon as I touch it.

However unfortunately that really doesn't matter as the phone is attached to a cord that is attached to the wall so that phone usually falls on the floor when it is touched because the cord is completely curled up and it is impossible to uncurl it.

Naturally I am then stuck with a no longer ringing phone on the floor and entangled in a mass of curled up cord as well as holding packages in my arms.

So much for that -then I go into my den which can be entered through the dinette as well as through the foyer. It also has a lovely terrace from which I can peek into the apartments of my neighbors in the building directly opposite me. Occasionally these people wave to me as a few of them are my friends.

This den also has a telephone which is on a book shelf which is behind a lamp and behind my bridge table as well, therefore the telephone is awkward to reach unless I am playing bridge.

Of course my fellow bridge players would prefer that I not answer that telephone during our bridge games.

To continue this saga, if I go back to the foyer and turn left, I can enter my very large living room, which is a most decidedly lovely space. It is filled with bibelots and ornaments as well as very nice furniture and in general it is considered to be quite attractive. In fact when a new guest arrives to see me, I usually point to that room and airily announce "and this is the living room!"

But the truth is that no one ever uses that room. It is just there on display. However it used to have 2 telephones but they were never used so they were ultimately discarded.

The next room is my office. Officially so. I have a computer, a telephone (land type) and an IPad and I am more or less content with my computer, although it keeps telling me to get cleaned up and very often it conks out entirely. Essentially though it sends my email promptly and I enjoy playing solitaire on it.

The telephone however has sporadic efficiency and as far as the IPad is concerned c'est un autre chose entirely. It hates me but it was presented to me for my last birthday by my wonderfully thoughtful children so I like it. It is a mini IPad with its own apple green suede cover, which is attached to it and keeps it closed, pristine and pretty.

But! I can't get anything on it! I open it and try to find the home page but no dice. I keep getting the same picture which gives me "app options" - none of which I would like. They only offer things like calendar, clock, ITunes and camera, so then I close it and then very slowly and sneakily I reopen it a little bit at a time. But the same thing keeps happening. However I do have a safety valve - her name is Patsy!

Now Patsy has been arriving at my apartment every weekday for the past 10 years at 8:00 AM promptly. If she is going to be even 10 minutes late she will call me and advise me of the delay. Also when she arrives she calls out "ting a ling" so I know she is at the door. I reply "ting" so she knows I'm alive.

The reason for this system is because a few years back I would call Patsy when she was in my apartment and ask "where are you?" She would then say "here". I would then ask "where is here "because I have so many rooms.

Therefore we decided it would be prudent for me to buy her a bell to hang around her neck, which would give me an inkling as to her whereabouts.

However unless it is Christmas time it is impossible to purchase a bell in any store so we devised the "ting a ling" arrangement which seems to work, because now I can find her.

At any rate Patsy is very savvy IPad wise, which sometimes irritates me because when I'm unable to move anything on my IPad, I turn it over to Patsy and instantaneously she gets it to work. This is most annoying to say the least. Otherwise she is very lovely to have around. In fact we may possibly go into a business partnership together making half sour pickles which we will call the B and P perfect pickle company. The initials of course are for our first names. (Also she tolerates my idiosyncrasies which is very kind of her).

At last - we now come to my bedroom at the very end of the apartment. This is my favorite room because it is very sunny and has a most comfortable chair in which I sit to write my books.

This chair in which I am sitting at present originally cost $29 in Peoria, Illinois when I first got married. Since that time it has been reupholstered 4 times, and what with the fabric cost, as well as the reupholstery charges, I probably have an investment in the chair of over $5000. So it has now become a very expensive item. Nevertheless I enjoy it to the utmost.

My bedroom also faces the La Guardia airport and I am able to see the arrival and departure of every airplane's comings and goings both day and night. I'm also far enough away so I don't hear their noise.

Did I mention my closets? They are plentiful, capacious, tidy and filled to the brim so all in all, l I'm extremely happy in my apartment. Do come and visit sometime!

MY BATHROOM MEMORIES

Recently while musing and reflecting upon events in my early life I came to the conclusion that my bathroom memories were at the forefront.

I distinctly recall my approximate age 4 at which time my head was blessed with a bountiful amount of curls, I sat myself down on our family toilet and with my mother's scissors in hand, I lopped off a goodly amount of those curls. Needless to say, this act was not appreciated by my mother, although the curls ultimately grew back.

Another time, at the same age, and being quite ill with a raging fever, my mother popped me into the bathtub in the same bathroom as the aforementioned event. The tub had been fully equipped with what was then known as Mustard Salts. This was considered to be a cureall for people who had high numbers on their thermometers. Apparently it was a successful treatment as I recovered completely in very short order.

Months later, but still aged 4 and at a different place entirely, I had another experience. This time we were visiting the country home of one of my father's sisters whom I considered to be quite formidable and I was generally leary when in her presence. This was because she had very strict rules as to all children's bodily functions when they were on her toilet.

Therefore while on this visit she escorted me to the bathroom and I was ordered to "perform". I protested vocally in a whiney manner and insisted vehemently that I did not have to "go".

Sticking to her convictions she proclaimed loudly that I had to sit there until nature took over.

I must admit that I was intimidated by her to the point of desperation. So I sat and sat and nothing positive occurred.

Finally my innate intelligence emerged and a brilliant solution was my salvation. I flushed the toilet! I then told my aunt that "success" had been achieved"!

We now proceed to my age 8 when I was a rather serious and curious minded child and therefore very much interested in how "things worked".

So one day while washing my hands in our bathroom sink, I kept wondering where the water (that was flowing onto me) emanated from. I then decided to investigate. Now the only way I presumed I would be able to do this, would be to insert my head in between the pipes behind the sink.

Well of course I was still unable to comprehend the intricacies of plumbing, even with my head back there, and then I came to the sad realization that I was completely stuck!

There I was in an untenable position. Naturally I screamed for help and luckily my mother and our housemaid tried to come to my rescue.

However even after their enthusiastic tugging and pulling, and plus my unabated screams as well, it was all to no avail so then it was decided that professional assistance was in order.

Therefore the fire department was called and about 5 of those stalwart individuals arrived lugging their hoses as well.

Unfortunately they too were unable to remove me and I was still thoroughly stuck! (Hopefully not forever!)

At last a plumber was summoned and sawed off one of the pipes. I was finally "out" and since then I thankfully have never put myself in such a position behind a sink. Behind the 8 ball yes!

My next bathroom adventure was at age 11. I had to go to the bathroom around 3am one night and when I walked in there I luckily turned on the light and realized I was not alone. There was a live mouse in the tub glaring at me---eek! I screamed and my father came running.

Heroically he grabbed the mouse by the tail and flushed it down the toilet.

Needless to say for many weeks afterwards I was nervous about using that toilet at night. I kept having visions of that mouse or maybe one of his relatives returning from a watery grave and possibly assailing me.

Gratefully I'm now pleased to say that since those early years my bathroom experiences have been quite normal.

MY DOCTOR

I have a general physician with an ever ready sense of humor, so it is quite pleasant when I am due for an appointment and can be treated to one of his snide type of jokes as well as worthwhile advice for any ailment I may have, all at the same time.

A week or so ago I was in his office and while he was reviewing a report pertaining to a brain scan I recently had in the office of another physician, my doctor said in a very comforting tone "well the good news is you have a "normal brain".

So as a contented patient I answered "isn't that nice that my brain is normal?

His reply was "yes, but the bad news is "you'll never be able to get a job in Congress".

MY KIDS

For some time now I've become aware of an absence of meaningful wordage relating to an important subject in any of my books.

In fact I realize that I've been thoroughly remiss in this regard, and therefore I wish to apologize.

Yes, I have absolutely neglected to mention my son Kenny in a loving fashion.

This son is truly a vital member of my family, and despite the fact that I have not mentioned him either kindly or often enough, this is to notify any of my readers that I absolutely do love him and that we are always on most compatible terms.

P.S. This is not to discount the fact that I have a wonderful daughter Nancy as well. And my love definitely applies to her also.

Signed (The Braggart)

MY LIFE IS AN OPEN BOOK

My life is an open book! Although not everyone can say the same thing. That is because everyone who has ever read any of my previous books definitely knows everything about <u>me</u>, although I don't necessarily know much about <u>them.</u>

Because

Some of these people have <u>Secrets</u>!

Now secrets are acceptable, especially if murder, incest, adultery, bigamy or any other unseemly or even criminal things have been committed by them.

But if just general information about a person's background has been kept in the dark, when it is possible that these facts could possibly be amusing, if known, or possibly a way of revealing that person's personality, then these so called secrets should be open and above board.

I personally know several people who have lots of secrets. They never tell you anything about themselves - where they were born (not in a good place?), where they went to school (never?)

Were their parents divorced? Evil? Fat? Ugly? From unknown countries? Brown? Black? Scarred? Midgets?, etc. We would really all like to know. Then we'd be able to know the <u>real</u> person.

However these people who hide the real them, always ask <u>you</u> (or me) personal questions which either one of us most likely answer truthfully. So is that fair?

Actually it is not that I care to know all the innermost and hidden facets about these people's lives, but on the other hand why do I have to tell them mine?

I suppose that is because I am unable to fib successfully and so therefore.....My life is an open book!

MY NEW LIFE

To those of you who may be interested, I wish to inform you that I now have a new name. My grandchildren presently refer to me as "Insta-<u>Gram!</u>"

This came about because I recently joined their popular website called "Instagram" and I have since placed many cryptic comments on it, where it is indicated to do so. Besides when these young ones post messages to their friends, I do also.

I am therefore considered to be a "friend" so my messages get through immediately and for some reason they think that I'm close to their ages, but also funny and perhaps weird!

I'm probably a little bit of each (except for the age) so I fit in perfectly.

However I do realize that my age group is not a usual one to be included in this site, but either I'm now in my second childhood or maybe I have a low I.Q., it doesn't seem to matter because we seem to have many things in common (my Instagram pals and me).

Incidentally some of the things they say about me are quite flattering such as "she's a genius" "she's out of this world", etc. So how can I resist my association with them?

Anyway I intend to continue writing on this site as long as I keep developing new followers.

MY PROBLEM

This is it! I've made up my mind I'm going to dehoard. Enough! I just came home from Florida and after unpacking all my luggage I found that there is no room in my closets to place them. Did I buy anything?

So then I tried on about 20 pairs of pants and they won't zip! How can that be? Is it because I've developed what is called a tummy! Oh God! I used to be a thin person, what happened?

And my cabinets! All filled with stuff! No wonder I write books about stuff! I'm an expert on stuff!

Papers! I have so many of them all small, all with writing on them but I can't seem to read what they say. Sometimes they seem to have telephone numbers of people unknown, sometimes email addresses, also of people I don't remember and sometimes a list of items I think I need to buy (which I don't need!)

What can I do! How do I get rid of these things? Help me, save me ! Anyone?

MY RESUME

I'm lucky enough to have a wonderful and talented granddaughter named Carly Zakin who founded a daily email web site called "TheSkimm.Com" along with another girl Danielle Weissberg. This web site has become extremely popular and the girls have been hiring additional people for their staff.

Recently Carly requested interested people to send in their resumes and on a lark I decided to send in mine.

She was much taken by my wordage but of course did not seriously consider me eligible for the job, nevertheless my resume still remains in her file, which I have now printed.

To whom It may concern:

I hereby offer my services to any and all interested parties (even those not interested).

My qualifications are as follows:

1. I don't drink, smoke or sleep on the job (except on weekdays).
2. I take minimum amounts of time for lunch breaks and for normal restroom visitations (except when I really have to go)

3. I smile often and nod my head in agreement even when I disagree with decisions made by higher-ups in the firm (which will probably be often.)
4. I wear attractive and well fitting attire with a demure aspect so far as colors are concerned (altho I'm partial to red, purple, green, yellow and pink all on one outfit).
5. I can type with the best of them (also with the worst).
6. I wear drugstore glasses (I'm cheap!)
7. I'm a Democrat (in moments of need)
8. I'm a Republican (under duress)
9. I'm usually an independent (for what it's worth)
10. My credit card is slightly overdrawn (I recently bought an airplane)
11. My bank account is nil but I'm hoping to get a salary soon (is this a paying job?)
12. I don't know anything about your company but I'm sure I'm right for this job)
13. Call me soon as I'm much in demand (oops! I forgot my e-mail address) (I'm old!)
14. When do I start?

BerniceZakin@aol.com
Also known as Insta-Gram

MY SIGHS FOR MY SIZE

My bras don't fit anymore. In fact I seem to be "bust"ing out all over.

I even think my sweaters and jackets are tight.

Is it possible that I have gained weight? How can that be? My scale is usually right although I haven't used it in some time.

The intake of my food hasn't seemed to change either, other than for the candy and cookies that I seem to be eating of late, but they are very small in size so they certainly should not cause a weight gain.

Of course, it is entirely possible that my clothing has definitely shrunk because the Chinese people who probably made them are at fault, as they are known to use inferior and skimpy fabrics, and besides they don't size their items correctly which no doubt results from our language barriers, so we "no comprendé" each other.

At any rate until we get back to making clothing in America again, I guess I'll have to buy larger sizes.

This Book May Be My Laster And Also My Worster Which Is Baddera Than Awfuler

"NEW" IS THE "NEW"

Presently there is a new and intriguing fad among the "ladies who lunch" in New York City.

These ladies are the first ones to adopt all nouveau fashion ideas which ultimately trickle down to the rest of America.

This latest craze is the one involving the application of vivid colors for finger tips and toe nails.

"Everyone"! I mean "everyone" is now having their finger nails painted in various tones and hues, ranging from black, purple, brown, orange, red, yellow, navy blue, green and silver.

In some instances designs and faces are also painted on them. In addition it is quite common to paint each nail a different color.

Toe nails are different. They are not supposed to match the finger nails. They are supposed to be a surprise element color wise to any foot fetishers, when they (the fetishers) are gaping at said toes.

These toes are usually completely visible under the 6" inch high heeled open toed sandals these fancy ladies wear, and all of <u>them </u>who go to elegant restaurants, couture shops, cocktail parties, and charitable organization festivities, as well as any other "<u>functions</u>", are then able to gape appreciatively and enviously at their friends gorgeous toes.

Because of this current fad, most nail salons cannot keep enough rich color toned polish bottles in stock, and the manufacturers of these polishes are therefore ecstatic.

Besides which, there are many foot doctors and dermatologists who can't wait to get hold of the many infected and misshapen feet that now exist, and are patiently waiting in the wings for new patients.

All in all most astute business people are looking forward to the next fad to hit the New York "fancy lady list". It will certainly mean large profits for all of them.

NEWS FLASH

Recently I read that America has lost its famous role as the leader of world advances in science, technology and math, etc.

In fact we have now been relegated to being No 2. Does that mean (according to the childhood definition of the word No. 2) that we are presently in a load of s—t?

NOBODY KNOWS ANYBODY

Recently a young friend of mine bemoaned the fact that her slightly Alzheimered mother no longer recognized her. Naturally she was devastated and needed comforting.

Luckily I was able to relieve her sadness by relating my own sorrowful situation. This usually comes about when I am having dinner with my own children and find that I too am unable to recognize <u>them</u>.

You see they are always intently gazing at their IPADS with their heads completely down and consequently the only thing I see are the <u>parts</u> in their hair (those that have hair) and since one <u>part</u> looks the same as any other, it is impossible to know who is whom.

My friend immediately felt better when I told her my own tale of woe.

NO FLY ZONE

What does it mean when "they" say people are dropping like flies"?

Does it mean that these people's season is over? (Flies usually fly in the summer).

Or does it also mean that people actually have a "season" in which they fall?

I can't believe <u>that</u> because in the North Shore Towers people fall and drop all the time regardless of the time of year.

So no doubt that expression is incorrect and "they" should no longer use it.

NO MORE

What shall I do now that I've stopped writing?

1. I will probably nibble more junk food.

2. I won't get up in the middle of the night to write what I am thinking. (But I'll still go to the bathroom).

3. I won't get ideas from what people around me discuss out loud.

4. I won't purchase any more writing stuff (i.e. pens, etc.)

5. I won't sit around contemplating anything.

6. I'll bore myself.

7. I'll sneakily think of writing another book.

NO THANK YOU
I'D RATHER STAY HOME

Rainy days are probably the best ones on my calendar. There is so much to do if I have to stay home because of the pelting drops.

Of course some friends may call and ask if I would like to play bridge or canasta, others may wonder if I would care to go to the movies or just visit with them.

However with the thunder clapping and loud downpours that I may hear outside my windows, I use them as an excuse to decline these options.

Instead I prefer not to move a muscle. I can just laze about. Maybe cuddle up with a cozy throw, and drink hot tea accompanied by a good book and several cookies. What a good time I would have!

I might even write a few nonsensical words (like these) or reminisce about the "good old days". Yes! They did exist!

Then too, there is a possibility that I'd call a few old friends (if any are left) who live in far away places, or perhaps nod my head and snooze.

But when I consider all these alternatives, I realize that I am probably aging because years ago I would have welcomed the rain which allowed me to dash off to Saks, Bloomies or other local stores and shop, shop, shop.

Today of course, as I have previously inferred, if anyone calls and offers various invitations, I simply say "no thank you, I'd rather stay at home".

OFF THEY GO

Once again there is the annual exodus from the 3 buildings in the North Shore Towers, of the Florida people who start returning to their southern climate residences.

They have all presumably and wearily packed the clothes they will never wear in Florida, and their clothing containers and boxes will most likely get expensively shipped south by various trucking companies.

Some things though are squooshed into their cars (those people who still drive) and those cars are either stuck on conveyances, or else private persons, such as retired airline pilots, drive them to their southern abodes.

Then when the Florida residents who are so exhausted from packing, say goodbye to their friends who are remaining at the North Shore Towers for the winter, they are quite smug and think "oh you poor things who are left to deal with the cold, snow and sleet for so many months"!

And those "poor ones" who are left at home envy the "smug ones" for a very short time, but then they are so happy that they didn't have to pack and that they would be warm and snugly at the Towers when the weather gets really bad.

The Florida guys on the other hand are enthusiastically happy for a short time, to see their full time Florida friends, even though it means unpacking and stocking up on groceries and sundries for the winter and making dates to get to so many different Boca places. Besides when it rains and gets cold in Florida (which it always does), they then envy their "stay at home" buddies.

Therefore on each succeeding winter less and less older individuals attempt to make the southern trek.

However there will always be upcoming younger ones who take their place, which is what is called the future and progress.

ONCE UPON A TIME

Once upon a time there was a great pair of shoes called Lefty and Righty. They were very expensive, hand made and most attractive. They lived on a shelf in a beautiful closet in a lovely apartment house located in the heart of New York, on Park Avenue no less.

They had medium heels, which meant that they could go any place comfortably. Also they were made of very fine leather in a neutral ebony tone and had a one of a kind unique buckle affixed to their front areas. In general they were always complimented upon whenever they were seen in public.

Mrs. Hartley Hartford the fourth, who was the lady who owned them, really adored them and consequently they were worn continuously. Therefore these shoes spent much of their time in the best restaurants, best clubs, and were also seen in the company of many extremely wealthy and socially famous people, as well as with other expensive, handmade and fine leather shoes; although none of these shoes ever had a unique buckle such as her pair.

One day however, while Mrs. Hartley Hartford the fourth was out shopping along Madison Avenue, Lefty tripped and slipped off Mrs. Hartley Hartford the fourth's foot, unfortunately cracking Lefty's heel during this episode.

So there they were in the middle of the day (thankfully after lunching in one of the best restaurants of the city) and in very dire circumstances. Righty felt terrible because now she had to bear the weight of Mrs. Hartley Hartford the fourth's discomforture, as Lefty was definitely out of commission.

Mrs. Hartley Hartford the fourth was frantic. She had made very exciting plans for this day. She had planned on visiting a "by invitation only" new very fancy dress shop "Upstairs on Madison" run by two very socially connected ladies, where they sold very expensive European clothing created by upcoming designers with great taste. The shop had a very fancy hand delivered and hand engraved invitation which was delivered by a houseman who was employed by one of the socially connected ladies who owned the new shop.

Also Mrs. Hartley Hartford the fourth anticipated having tea with <u>the</u> Mrs. Van der Couple the third (an extremely wealthy friend) at Mrs. Van der Couple the third's extremely gorgeous home with other extremely wealthy ladies. It was going to be an extremely lovely day.

Now of course, these exciting plans had to change. Lefty of course was not to blame. It was an accident, but as a result Righty was the "Sole" shoe left in Mrs. Hartley Hartford the fourth's possession.

What course could Mrs. Hartley Hartford the fourth now pursue? Ah! At last a glimmer of hope emerged! There was a well known "shoe fix it store" quite nearby called "Jim's".

If Mrs. Hartley Hartford the fourth could manage to limp over to that store then possibly "Jim" or one of this "shoe'ers" could repair Lefty. Righty too was anxious to have such a terrible weight removed from this dire situation.

So Mrs. Hartley Hartford the fourth frantically hobbled over to "Jim's" (just three blocks away) and after a consultation with the experts, she was graciously escorted to a little booth where Lefty was removed from her presence, and where Mrs. Hartley Hartford the fourth could relax while the restoration to perfect "shoedom" to Lefty could take place.

This was promised to happen within the hour. Therefore Mrs. Hartley Hartford the fourth had fond hopes of being able to complete her very exciting plans for the day, before returning home to her lovely apartment on Park Avenue, where the newly repaired Lefty and the stalwart Righty could again be returned to their beautiful closet shelf.

So everything was ultimately fine and "Jim's" shop proved to be the magic solution.

Therefore Mrs. Hartley Hartford the fourth was happy once again, and was able to buy 3 dresses at the new "Upstairs on Madison Avenue Shop" where they sell very expensive clothing crafted by upcoming designers from Europe.

Then of course she had tea with Mrs. Van der Couple the third, her extremely wealthy friend, along with those other extremely wealthy ladies who were all having tea at Mrs. Van der Couple the third's extremely gorgeous home at the same time. Mrs. Hartley Hartford the fourth finally was able to go home to her lovely apartment in the heart of New York on Park Avenue.

Naturally after that sad incident, the newly repaired Lefty and the stalwart Righty went back on their shelf in their beautiful closet in the same apartment.

The End

"ON THE OTHER HAND"

Did you ever wonder how that expression came to pass? Well I did - It actually came to my mind just the other day. I was curious as to whether any person actually ever had an additional hand - like three of them.

This isn't so illogical because I once knew someone whose brother-in-law had six toes on one foot, and another person (a friend of my parents) who had two thumbs (side by side) on one hand.

The person who had two big toes on his one foot probably had to have all his shoes made to order just to accommodate that extra toe, which no doubt was a big expense. If it had been the pinky toe, he could have just squished it into a regular shoe. Luckily though he was very financially successful so I guess it didn't matter how much he spent on his shoes.

Now the person I knew with the two thumbs was quite proud of the extra one. He was always showing it off, even though at one time it was suggested that he have it removed. He never did so however.

It recently occurred to me though that he must have had a problem with gloves, since the extra thumb had no place to go in a glove. Therefore it (the thumb) must have been very cold in the winter time.

He could possibly have moved to Florida so he would not need gloves, but actually he remained in New York so I presume his wife may have knit some gloves for him with an extra digit. Or maybe still he could have cut a thumb portion off another glove, and stuck it on his extra thumb when it got very cold outside - I never knew. By the way, I think he felt he was too old for mittens.

Coming to think of it, most little children who were thumb suckers, would probably loved to have an additional one. Then if the one thumb on each hand got <u>over sucked</u>, that child could use the one in reserve!

Since the two thumbed man I knew passed away so many years ago, I never had the opportunity to ask him how he managed to keep that extra one warm in the winter.

Ironically he had a very lucrative business, he made the <u>skin coverings</u> for all kosher hot dogs. In a way you might think that was wishful thinking for <u>covering</u> up his additional thumb. "On the other hand" (ha ha), I don't know if there was any connection.

OVER HEARD

I recently went to my Doctor's office as I had some kind of virus and when the nurse asked me why I was there, I answered truthfully in a whisper, "because I lost my voice and can't talk".

There was a gentleman sitting nearby obviously waiting to see the doctor and when he heard what I whispered he mumbled under his breath "I wish that would happen to my wife".

PREVENTIVE MEDICINE

It is safe to say that the average person is usually advised that visiting various physicians on a yearly basis, is a way of insuring that their good health is maintained. It may also help to prolong life and avoid any physical mishaps that might occur if these visits do not take place.

Therefore as a dutiful advocate of the large groups of people who are mindful of such good advice, I make it my business to have a yearly series of appointments with all the doctors whose specialties relate to my own physical being.

Along the way, during these numerous visits, I am poked, prodded, and peered at and practically turned upside down, hoping that these maneuvers will result in my achieving a "clean bill of health". However I have yet to discover if there is such a thing as "dirty bill of health".

At any rate, even though I have been to the offices of quite a few different specialists throughout these many years (not that I am a hypochondriac) I have yet to visit a physician who specializes in "belly buttons" - or at least nobody has ever evinced any interest in mine.

So I've wondered - does any doctor ever specialize in them? Is it better to have an "innie" or an "outie"? Should either type be examined yearly? Have all my doctors been neglectful for not examining mine? Should I worry that all of my doctors have avoided such scrutiny? I certainly would be interested in finding out if I am up to standard belly button wise.

Another thing that bothers me is the fact that when I receive a medical prescription on one of the forms physicians use, it is impossible to read what it says. I actually queried one of my doctors the other day about this dire situation. I asked him point blank whether it was because the doctor did not want his patient to know the contents of what was written. I also wanted to know whether it was written in a special medical code and if students in medical school had to take a particular course in order to learn how to write these very sneaky prescriptions. My doctor innocently replied by indicating that in his case he had to write so much that it was easier to scribble, and that so far as he knew all pharmacists seemed able to interpret his scrawl.

His answer satisfied me, but I am still worried about my belly button as I believe that as a dedicated medical patient, I'm entitled to know the truth!

REPUBLICAN ROGUES

Ted Cruz, Paul Ryan, Rand Paul
You think you three know it all
You're impressed with your thinking
But I think it's stinking
And believe you are due for a fall

Though your politics now lean to the right
We hope you'll soon see the light
And for the next "Potus"
You'll cede to "Dem" voters
And give up without a big fight

Of course I know T'will be Tough
As you guys really like to play rough
But "GOPs" are big flops
And the "Dems" are now tops
So face it - <u>you</u> don't have the <u>stuff</u>!

SECRETS

When I think back to my early childhood I realize it contained many unusual secrets.

Now most little children in my lifetime enjoyed fairly normal experiences filled with every day activities, such as games, toys, school, family get togethers and friends.

However when I was about nine years old my childhood changed considerably. By that I mean that in addition to engaging in the above activities, both my older sister and I became our mother's confidante and frequently our times together became filled with the titillating episodes in the life of my mother's closest friend. Our mother related these sordid tales to us daily at great length as no doubt she wanted to unburden herself.

This friend apparently came from a very well known New York City family and her husband was a noted attorney. His brother held a prominent role in the music world, and her two sons were equally famous in the radio and broadcasting fields as well.

She was an unassuming, not particularly attractive, overweight woman who was adept in both knitting and crocheting. In fact she taught me how to do both and seemingly occupied her time with making beautiful items such as dresses, suits, sweaters, bed throws, etc. A person would never suspect that she had an alter ego.

Nevertheless she led a very secret life. She was a nymphomaniac and indulged in extremely weird sexual behavior.

Since my mother didn't trust anyone else among her acquaintances with the revelation of her friend's confessions and the fact that this lady apparently needed someone in whom she could confide, and had selected my mother for that role, it was only logical that my mother chose my sister (9 years older than I was) and me to become the recipients of these ongoing tales of this lady's lurid escapades.

I particularly recall being at a hotel in Asbury Park when my mother confided that her friend, who was also a guest there at the same time, told my mother that she had several liaisons with one of the bell hops, whom she befriended when he delivered her luggage. Since her husband played golf daily, he was conveniently absent when she was indulging in her dalliances with this young man! Her descriptions of these times were vivid and even though I was quite young I understood what was happening.

A year or so later my mother gave us a sequel to her friend's personal life. It seems that this time she met a taxicab driver enroute to someplace or other and subsequently spent many months having an affair with him.

Also every Friday afternoon she went to the Roseland Dance Hall where weekly dances were held and she usually hooked up sexually each Friday with any convenient dancing partner.

This lady was not selective, she was simply hungry for risky indulgences with unknown men who were definitely not in her social circle.

Needless to say these racy relationships were eagerly listened to by my sister and myself and my mother's sexy friend was totally unaware that anyone other than my mother knew her secrets, least of all two young girls.

Then when I was about 13 in my first year of High School, a good friend who was in the same class, related lurid tales about her father. It seems that he had fathered 2 illegitimate children whom she never met and who lived in Europe.

One day she brought into the classroom a book of drawings her father had drawn. He was a renowned scenic designer and this book, which she surreptiously showed to several of her classmates, contained extremely graphic pictures of sexual acts. I must admit this was my first awareness of such behavior and it was most enlightening to say the least.

Again when I was about 16 another good friend who was quite sophisticated and daring, confided that she had indulged in two sexual experiences - one at a sleep away camp and another with a total stranger while on a railroad train enroute to Florida.

In those years this behavior was unheard of and I had to pretend that I wasn't shocked although I most certainly was.

A year later this girl married one of our high school teachers, a union that lasted about 2 years. Then a year later I introduced her to her second husband with whom she had a son.

Sorrowfully that marriage fell apart a few years later, whereupon I lost track of her although I subsequently found out that she had remarried, and then divorced that man, and then married him again for just a few years.

Several years later I discovered that she had purchased a house with another woman and as far as I know they've been together about 25 years. What their personal relationship is I'm not sure although I have many suspicions.

The last secret I'm about to reveal is most unusual. I was an interior designer for about 35 years and during that time I did business with a particular lady on a frequent basis.

We became quite friendly during which time she told me her life story.

I knew she was quite wealthy apart from her very successful business and one day she explained how this occurred.

It seems that when her European mother was about 16 and still living in a small foreign country (I never knew which one) she had an illicit affair with a prince and as a result she had a baby (my business friend). Naturally the prince did not marry her but he paid for her to move to America and purchased about 100 acres of land in (at that time) an unknown area of the Hamptons, for her as well.

This property of course increased considerably in value through the years and consequently this lady acquired great wealth.

She also told me that when she was about 5 years old she recalled meeting her father (the prince) at the Plaza and sitting on his lap at lunchtime. Of course she was unaware of the relationship- simply that he seemed to be a nice man.

Her mother married a few years later and had another daughter who never knew that her older sister (and my business friend) did not have the same father, even though the two girls worked together for 50 years. She confided that I was the only person to whom she ever told about her early life.

This same lady also told me another strange tale. As I mentioned before, she was very successful in business and as a result she was invited to the White House to meet and have dinner with the then president of the United States. This came about because she was a pioneer in her field.

Unfortunately this resulted in a rather complicated situation as during her early married life (her then husband was stationed in Europe for awhile) and she and her husband frequently had dinner and socialized with the man who ultimately became a president as well as his steady girl friend.

Therefore when she got to the White House and was introduced to the president he asked "don't I know you" whereupon she tactfully said "no I just have a familiar face".

However she further related that all during dinner he kept glancing at her with a quizzical expression, but of course she did not want to embarrass him about his illicit girl friend way back in Europe.

Since all these people have now passed away, I feel comfortable revealing these unseemly tales.

But for a person who has always led a fairly ordinary, modest and exemplary life I certainly have managed to harbor many sordid secrets.

SHE KNOWS IT ALL

My daughter Nancy is a very astute person and is generally a font of information.

In fact many of her friends are completely anxious for her aid in helping them solve their shopping problems. Also she usually knows the answer to many questions commonly in need of correct answers.

You might say that she has the reputation of being very <u>street</u> savvy.

The trouble is that only very few of these people know which <u>streets</u> we are discussing.

As far as I know her preferences are 5th Avenue, Park Avenue and Madison Avenue and the actual street numbers range from the 70's to the 50's.

I doubt seriously if her "know how" goes beyond these perimeters, although I don't intend this to be a derogatory statement. It simply infers that she is rarely to be found outside these boundaries.

Nancy is also an avid "walker" and therefore she is completely able to advise everyone within her circle, which store sells what and what is the key item to purchase or identify.

Call her anytime. She <u>may</u> answer and you'll be astounded as to how much you will learn.

SHOWERS

Of course everyone has heard of baby showers, bridal showers and engagement showers but not so many people are aware of meteor showers.

Now at a meteor shower I guess all the constellations are invited, sort of like "are the stars out tonight" kind of event, at which "the sky is the limit".

Naturally no boxed gifts are given or received when this event occurs but in a way the world receives a special kind of gift and "god" knows what that is.

SORDID REVELATIONS

Gloria Phillips was beautiful - really beautiful. She had flawless skin, a perfectly arched nose - huge blue eyes with luscious long lashes highlighting them, a radiant smile and a magnificent figure with model like contours. She was a delight to behold and strangers were always awed by her magnificent appearance.

But her close friends and of course members of her immediate family had a decidedly different perception of her.

You see Gloria had a secret -she had undergone many, many cosmetic procedures which naturally enhanced her entire being. As a result she clearly resembled a person far younger than her actual age, which was 80.

Some people however did suspect what she had done to achieve such a fantastic physical appearance, but of course no one in her family or her few very close friends would ever reveal the truth about her.

Nevertheless as time elapsed several of Gloria's old friends passed away and when Gloria attended their funerals many people who were present presumed Gloria must have been a daughter of one of the deceased! Otherwise they could not understand why such a young person would attend the services of an older person.

All was fine for several years, during which time Gloria's new friends who were so much younger than she was, were perplexed by the fact that her appearance never changed. They figured she just had wonderful genes and also believed that she was much younger than they were.

Suddenly though in her late 90's Gloria developed several physical ailments. She had back trouble, heart and blood pressure problems, and in general her health declined rapidly.

So when at 97 years old she passed away, still looking young and beautiful. These much younger new friends viewed her body at the funeral and they all sadly commented upon the fact that their beautiful friend had died at such "a young age".

Little did they know that in fact Gloria could easily have been a grandmother to some of them.

Thus she was able to carry her secret to her grave.

However the strangest thing of all was that there were many cosmetic surgeons at the service, none of whom knew each other, nor did they know that Gloria had been a frequent patient to all of them. Since they each performed different surgeries on her, she was never recognized when she arrived at their offices for another surgery and then they all thought she was a new patient, and one who now would represent a steep financial loss to all of their medical practices.

TELLING TALES

I suppose I should not be telling tales about other people but in this case I thought the story was so funny that I decided to reveal it.

Two ladies were having lunch in a restaurant a few years ago and while enjoying their salads or whatever, one lady remarked that the gentleman a few tables away looked familiar.

The other lady persuaded her friend to find out if indeed she knew him.

So the first lady sent a note through the waiter in which she asked "are you from Texas"?

Shortly afterwards she received a reply in this manner. He lifted his leg high in the air to indicate Texas boots.

Whereupon the first lady who had a very good sense of humor said to her companion, "it's a good thing I didn't ask him if he was Jewish"!

THE AMERICAN OBSESSION WITH FIREARMS INVADES OUR CONVERSATIONS

He is always <u>shooting</u> his mouth off

She's really a <u>pistol</u>

Don't <u>gun</u> your motor

Be careful in a <u>revolving</u> door

"<u>Bullets</u> over Broadway" is a great show

It's important to <u>aim</u> for the future

How about another <u>round</u>?

<u>Charge</u> it!

What <u>triggered</u> that remark?

Don't be a big <u>shot</u>!

This Book May Be My Laster And Also My Worster Which Is Baddera Than Awfuler

THE BATTLE IS ON

Have any of you seen the television advertisement that advises men to "guard their manhood's?" I have and it makes me wonder if it intimates that a sentry should be posted in the front of every male person.

It never actually says so but I believe that this advertisement thinks that most men are in danger of being attacked by women. Therefore I imagine that the Band-Aid protection they recommend is not the answer to their problem.

So perhaps women have finally come into their own and men had better beware. Maybe it is time for all our ladies to go on the offensive and denounce those manhood's entirely.

In fact we must safeguard our womanhoods. Yes! We must strike against invasion!

THE BIG DAY

Here it is the Sunday on which we consumers are expected to push our clocks forward and forfeit an important hour of our lives that formerly was utilized for extra sleep, or other important activities which demanded our time.

That hour belonged to us and was our absolute possession, and we as United States citizens insist upon the return of what was rightfully ours.

Of course the nasty bureaucrats who created this time change are just trying to loll us into thinking that the missing hour would bring more daylight and sunshine into our lives and they promise to return it in the fall of the year.

Nevertheless this does not rectify our present situation or the dilemma in which we find ourselves.

We (I mean me in particular) are absolutely in need of that extra hour right now!

For instance I cannot wait until October to call a friend in Arizona where there is no time change.

And I also do not wish to give up eating my breakfast in order to arrive at my hair dressing establishment (which now observes the new time change) in order <u>not</u> to be tardy for my appointment.

There are many other obligations that I have which require my extra hour so I repeat...I want my hour back right now!

THE "BRIDGE" OF SIGHS

It is a known fact that I get the most awful cards when I play bridge, which is 2 to 3 times a week, and which also means that I am thoroughly miserable on those days and that all my partners hate to play opposite me as well.

Now those of you who play bridge can sympathize with my situation, when I tell you that I usually never have more than 2-5 points in each hand. Awful! N'est pas? Awful! In English too.

Therefore when I play, everyone in my games is most unhappy, because I whine, complain and moan constantly. When I do this my partners look at the other people who are playing opposite us with helpless expressions, as if to say "we are stuck with her". Sometimes they actually pretend to be ill or have toothaches, just so they can legitimately leave the game and go home, hoping to never play with me again. Occasionally this works because I notice that I hardly ever play with the same people if they can avoid it.

But on occasion! I do get good cards! Mind you this is seldom but! It does happen, and then I don't necessarily know how to bid, because I'm so used to passing.

Anyway the other day I really picked up a gorgeous hand and I hardly knew how to bid (as I told you this happens so seldom).

But then I glowed and beamed with pride and actually got up the courage to bid "two no trumps", which is a really "big deal" (this is related to the way the cards are dealt) and guess what?! My partner <u>passed</u> me! Almost unheard of, but she couldn't help it. She had what is known as a Yarborough (one of my old hands). She had absolutely no points - nada - zero - sad!

Justifiably I came to the sorrowful conclusion that the bridge god hates me and probably always will.

So now I'm taking canasta lessons and I think I have the possibility of making some new card playing friends. That is if I pick the pack and get some wild cards!

THE CARD ROOM

I believe that the card room where I live is a most unusual place. Many ladies (mostly in foursomes) play cards there regularly, and particularly on the weekends.

The games themselves (bridge, canasta and maj jong) are not the important forms of amusement taking place however. In fact "chatter, gossip and companionship" are the major activities.

The "chatter" is fairly general, such as "where are you going tonight?" "Are all of your children married?" "Did you hear about the bad weather we expect tomorrow"? These and other mundane subjects are usually discussed.

However the "gossip" is entirely different. In fact it is really the most important item on the agenda of the majority of the ladies in that room.

It usually goes something like this "did you realize that <u>she</u> is "losing it"? "Have you heard that "so and so" has a new boyfriend", "you know the one that just moved in and she immediately put her hooks in him". Also, "I just heard that so and so fell and broke her hip and I understand she'll be in rehab for a month and then she is going to hire my old aide". Further comments include "boy she sure is getting fat and look at those wrinkles", or "she used to live in my old neighborhood and had the worst reputation" and finally "what do you think my apartment is worth now" and "guess what, I may move to Florida".

Of course there are many other subjects being discussed but the most frequent ones are the aforementioned.

Mind you, not much money is either won or lost, however in retrospect the card room is not so unusual after all <u>and</u> the companionship is terrific!

THE COUPLE

Several weeks ago I was on the third avenue bus and was luckily able to get a seat next to the window.

Right in front of me there was a very attractive lady sitting alone after the person next to her left the bus.

When that happened a man who had been sitting way in the back suddenly dashed down to join her and they started conversing rapidly.

At that point I realized that they probably had been old friends or were even romantically involved.

At any rate she was very tiny while he was at least a head or so taller. They were very clubby and in the midst of their animated conversation he suddenly fixed a loose tendril of her hair and adjusted her dress collar. She in turn straightened his tie and seemed to pat the handkerchief in his pocket as if to make it look better.

They then whispered to each other and laughed hilariously. Of course I could not hear a word they said though I tried, nevertheless they were very compatible although she seemed to be a bit too old for him.

He seemed to be about 20 years younger but of course in today's world that would hardly be a deterrent to a relationship even though they did seem ill matched.

Then just as I was getting ready to leave the bus, he suddenly rose from his seat also and kissed her tenderly on the cheek. His final words which I did hear were goodbye Mom, have a nice day!

THE EARLY ME

According to my vital statistics, I was born in 1865 and once had an unusual dream about some remarkable inventions that seemingly were to occur in the future.

It really didn't seem possible but in the dream there appeared to be something called radio where a person could actually hear another person whose voice came out of a box. Can you imagine?

And then there was a similar happening named television whereby that person in the box could actually be <u>seen</u> as well as heard.

Also events that were taking place at the <u>present</u> or the past were able to be witnessed by the owners of these television sets (as they were called).

These incredible things seemed to be prevalent in my dreams and there were numerous other inventions that really didn't seem possible.

Just think, you could actually have a conversation with someone who lived in Paris, London, or even Australia just by pushing different numbers on a device called "telephone"

I must say these impossible inventions appeared to be daily occurrences in my dream and when I woke up I thought how wonderful it would be to live in that kind of future world.

Do you think it will ever happen?

THE EMPEROR HAS NO CLOTHES
OR
THE BULLY IN THE SCHOOL YARD

I am of course referring to "Cruz" who does not deserve to be called "Senator Cruz" but the two titles above fit him to a "T".

This man is a nouveau arrival in Washington but actually is a born Canadian. I do believe that in his black heart he loves his "North of the Border" ties, who scoffs at Americans and feels it is incumbent upon him to bring Washington to its knees.

Whether he will ultimately be successful is still unknown at this juncture (the present time is October 2013).

Hopefully Washington and all the non kooks who still exist there will come to its senses and once again be able to allow our country to resume sensible daily operations.

In retrospect I wonder how the founding fathers would judge the politicians of today. Would they consider Republicans to be arrogant fools who completely ignore "Majority Rules" or that they themselves failed to enact the proper laws to prevent such "Cruz Stupidity".

THE END?

The world as we know it is fast disappearing.

Ironically we are suffering the extinction of our planet due to global overpopulation, and at the same time we are also sadly lamenting the obesity of our children, which in a way is kind of a "two for one" situation.

In other words one obese person is equal to two regular sized people. Therefore the total amount of our existing populace is being "doubled".

This represents a disaster previously unknown to mankind, which brings to mind this question. "How can we possibly house, clothe, feed, cure or otherwise care for the ongrowing abundance of humans on our planet in the ensuing years?

In addition we must also acknowledge the fact that our rivers keep rising, our icebergs are melting and our climate is rapidly changing for the worse.

These occurrences actually help to <u>diminish</u> our population which is the antithisis to the <u>over</u>population problem. But on the other hand, newfound medical inventions are keeping more people alive!

So how do we rectify this weird <u>opposing</u> set of circumstances and which would be the proper choice for most of us.

"Do we want to prolong life for more people, or do we wish to live comfortably on our earth that is only equipped to provide amply for a limited amount of inhabitants?"

Was God apparently on the side of a lesser amount of earthly beings when he foretold of pestilence, floods, toads and many other biblical plagues which would certainly reduce the existence of too many people? Or was he simply explaining what could happen?

Nevertheless the "right to lifers" want us to increase our numbers ad infinitum.

So what is actually the correct solution? I guess most of us will either never know or else we may make the wrong decision or (hopefully the right one?)

The only people who might have definite preferences are probably the undertakers and the obstetricians.

THE "INSIDE" STORY

In a recent issue of the New Yorker magazine, I saw a cartoon that reached the very core of me. It was drawn by a person initialed R.Cha "something" and indicated two egg persons marveling at their insides (which appeared to be what looked like fried eggs slightly underdone).

This certainly got me thinking about my own insides. Naturally I have more stuff inside me than what was indicated by the insides of the cartoon's egg persons, but to tell the truth I am unable to name <u>everything</u> within <u>me</u>.

Of course I know that I have two kidneys, bladder, a liver, a heart, two ovaries plus many other unnameables.

This thought in itself is remarkable when I think that all day long I walk around with more inside me than outside me.

Actually I've never seen my insides but I have to wonder if these organs like each other. Are they jealous of each other's role in handling my daily life?

For instance does my heart think it's more important than my bladder? I would think that both of them carry an equal amount of weight in my body, and I'm not talking pound wise.

I actually manage to keep my bladder busy all day and night, and thank goodness I presently have complete control over it.

But my heart is really working on its own. My liver seems to manage by itself too, however I believe my ovaries think they've had their day.

All in all my insides seem to be quite compatible and I certainly hope they will continue to be so, until I have no need for any of them, i.e. when I reach my termination period.

THE OLD NEIGHBORHOOD

The trip down memory lane is very often a meaningful and pleasant one. It is also a time when it sometimes possible for a person to recollect many past events, as well as where they took place as well.

In my long ago I can vividly recall my various neighborhood streets, including many of the stores that existed from 72nd street and Broadway to 96th street and Broadway. Also the lovely area from Riverside Drive on the Hudson River to Central Park West and Central Park itself is still one of my fondest remembrances.

This little section before World War II was like a small town. Most of the inhabitants (mainly Jewish) knew each other, usually their children attended the same schools, and the parents generally shopped in the same stores.

86th Street and Broadway was really the hub. There was the subway entrance on the north west corner with a newsstand right next to it, where it was possible to buy all the best magazines, newspapers from all foreign countries, and song sheets that had the words to all the popular songs of the day.

Children (particularly me) were able to buy these sheets for 5 cents, and then walk home merrily singing the words to the tunes we all knew so well.

Luckily too, several museums (on the east side) were fairly close to our dwellings, where young people were fortunately able to acquire a good deal of artistic knowledge at an early age and <u>free</u> of charge.

Again in those years most items (whether they were food, clothing or entertainment) had very low prices compared to today's exorbitant ones.

I distinctly recall a loaf of freshly baked bread from Tiptoe Inn costing 9 cents and the nearby subway ride was 5 cents as was the trolley car fare.

A pair of lovely shoes at A.S. Beck on 83street was $3.95 and an expensive handbag at Davids next door to Becks was $10. Schraafts delicious sundaes covered with hot butterscotch or hot chocolate toppings with crisp almonds were 35 cents and orchestra seats for Broadway shows were $3.95. Neighborhood movie theaters offered first run films for 15 cents. These were certainly bargain prices compared to the ones today.

Best of all the Chinese restaurant upstairs on 86th street and Broadway over Tiptoe Inn (the best restaurant on the west side) served a complete lunch which included soup, egg roll, main dish and dessert for 35 cents, wow!

Ellman's, a coffee shop on that block was also a great place to have a soda after a young person's first date at a movie.

In my day this neighborhood was a magical place and I wish it existed today!

THE REAL ME

Hello everyone. I would like to introduce myself. I'm a bagel, which is kind of a round tasty type of roll. I'm sometimes fat, sometimes a little flatter, and I often arrive in chip form.

My forebears were European, in fact quite Schtetyly, although now I am thoroughly Americanized, but definitely Jewish, even though of late my religious affiliations have changed drastically.

Indeed I have suddenly become quite interracial. I am comfortable with Catholics, and Protestants, and even Muslims, despite the fact that they (the Muslims) generally keep their interest in me hidden away.

They actually make believe that I don't exist, that I'm a bakery error and they tend to circulate false statements inferring that I am just an Israeli figment of the Jewish imagination, although in private they might be willing to concede that I am delicious.

However this attitude does not discourage me personally, as I am perfectly content to hang around with my good friends cream cheese and Nova Scotia salmon.

Also when I'm placed on a buffet table I disappear immediately which certainly proves my popularity. As you can see, I am adaptable with many varying sects, and on many holiday occasions, including Christmas.

Recently I have also branched off into several distinct personalities taste wise. I can be a sesame type, or an onion type, or even a caraway seed type. Can you imagine such a divergence in- let's say -a doughnut? - Absolutely not!

Therefore it is safe to assume that I am unique and would enthusiastically suggest that you serve me as your favorite item at any meal, either as a first course, appetizer, or even as an entrée.

By this time I am sure you realize wholeheartedly that I am delectable and also <u>cheap</u>!

THE SEAT OF LUXURY

Recently my daughter Nancy who usually calls me every day to check on my well being, found out that I was unable to answer her call due to my being otherwise occupied. So shortly afterwards when I retrieved her call I said "you know Nancy there are times when a person has to go to the bathroom".

She replied "oh I have someone who does that for me". I then asked her "how often does that person come to your house"? She answered "3 times a week", so I asked which days and she replied, "Tuesday, Thursday, and Friday" at which point I hung up. But then a little later I called her back and queried "how much does that service cost"? "I think I might be interested". Her reply at that time was "I really don't know I put it on my credit card". I did not call her again.

THE SECRET IS OUT

The secret of a long marriage is very simple.

1. Marry someone who is constantly on the road trying to sell things to people far away.

2. When that husband occasionally returns home, be sure to recognize him. Cook a nice dinner and then pretend to have a nervous breakdown. He will then return to his mother's home for other meals.

3. If he resumes his business trips you will have plenty of time to play bridge, shop and go to the movies, etc.

4. If you are very lucky this arrangement may continue for several years.

5. Ultimately, lots of time will pass and you both can make plans to have a huge 50th wedding anniversary party.

6. At the party no doubt all the guests will wish you well and compliment you both on your being together for so many years.

7. Thus you will have finally solved the secret of a long marriage.

THE WHINER

I don't like to whine, in fact I try to willingly accept the inevitable in a kindly and respectful manner.

However there are occasions when I feel it is imperative to voice my honest opinions and displeasure.

And today is one of those times. I am absolutely, positively annoyed beyond words. In fact I am pissed! (But don't tell anyone I said a bad word).

You see, in good faith I tried to reinstate myself with "Twitter". Mind you I don't use "Twitter" on a regular basis. Actually I have never tweeted at all, however I do receive Tweets occasionally from my children and grandkids, who are all "tech savvy". I on the other hand, am definitely <u>not</u>!

Nevertheless I thought I should get back on "Twitter" (some of my grandchildren put me there originally) as apparently I expired! No I didn't die, but they kicked me out and in order to reconnect with my family I tried to rejoin and get back into Twitter's good graces.

Well I soon found that it was utterly impossible! They wanted so much information it was absurd, truly ridiculous.

I put in my password (I thought it was my password) about 8 times, no dice. I then put in my telephone number, again, no dice! I kept putting in so much stuff about myself that I actually did not recognize me at all. In fact I wished it wasn't me.

And unfortunately I also found out that it is necessary to have different passwords for every electronic device or app and also to put those words in a safe place wherever that might be.

That whole idea is really crazy because maybe someday we might need passwords for everything we do. Supposing we want to order dinner in a restaurant, the waiter might possibly say "what's your password and if you forget the right one, you could starve to death!

Anyway I was now in a cold sweat! I hated all my electronics stuff. Why do I need a computer, TV, IPad, IPhone and 6 regular phones when all I want is to sit back quietly, read a good book and eat my pickles.

Frankly I am just a simple person, I don't belong in this generation. It is filled with evil people who only communicate with machines so why don't I just forget the whole tech world. I'd probably never fit in with the "techies" anyway.

Therefore don't try to tweet me either because I won't answer. If by some chance I do answer and you ask for my password, I'll say "I don't know" (which will be my password)!

THINGS ARE NOT ALWAYS WHAT THEY SEEM TO BE INITIALLY

Have any of you people out there ever given a thought as to the prominence of today's fixation for initials?

Indeed there apparently is an unquestionable fondness for them and their usage, particularly among younger individuals. Older personages are <u>almost</u> and I must say <u>almost</u> as predisposed to include them in their speech as well.

Be way of explanation I mean that during a goodly amount of conversation today, it is quite usual to hear people say what the f--k or oh sh-- instead of the uttering of the fully lettered words that these initials indicate.

The one exception perhaps is the mention of the <u>N</u> letter usually referred to as the <u>N</u> word. This word has a connotation that is more evil than obscene and is not generally used conversationally, although it may be done so negatively.

By that I am inferring that people <u>will</u> use it by saying "do <u>not use</u> the <u>N</u> word", whereas the letters F and Sh are definitely uttered very frequently instead of using other adjectives. By the way these two may also be used as nouns.

It is not possible to determine how this curtailment of fully lettered words came to pass. Certainly it was not to save paper while writing, nor to save time while speaking. In fact quite the opposite.

I believe it was simply meant to emphasize what a person wished to convey thus using initials seemed to be appropriate.

I personally do not adhere to this popular form of talking <u>initially</u> because I would prefer to think of myself as a wordsmith.

However as my late husband used to say "she (referring to me) wouldn't say sh-- even if she had a mouthful".

THIS IS A FERRY TALE

Once upon a time in the very long ago there lived a little girl who grew up in a big town called "Manhattan".

Now this town was surrounded by water. There was a river on the east side and there was another river on the west side.

The river on the west side was quite unusual. Very often it had several large boats that were docked there, until they acquired passengers who were anxious to sail to Europe, which was known to be a very wonderful place indeed.

In addition this river had something else called ferry boats, on which passengers could sail to a place called New Jersey just across the river for only five cents a ride.

People could either ride in their cars for their trip or just sit on benches inside the cabin that were provided for that purpose.

This was really quite a bargain price wise, although at that time five cents was actually a considerable sum of money.

At any rate very often a young man would be able to invite a young lady of his choice to accompany him for an evening ride on one of the ferry boats.

This was what was known as "a cheap date", a common expression in those days (also known as the depression era).

Now that little girl about whom we mentioned in the first paragraph was fortunate enough to be invited on just such a date when she became a teenager, and the young man who invited her to join him on that occasion, became her first beau.

Naturally she never forgot that initial ferry ride date, but many years later when she was really a grown up married lady, she went to that far way place called Europe many times.

However it was usually in a new invention called an aeroplane and it cost a lot of money.

On those trips she and her husband (a prince of a fellow) had wonderful times and they both lived happily thereafter.

THIS IS A POEM

This is a poem
It is the voice of a lover
The sound of the ocean
The cry of a baby
The tweet of a bird
It has no rhyme
And no reason
It just is

TIME FLIES

The above is absolutely an absurd statement. Anybody with a modicum of sense has to know that "<u>time</u>" simply indicates a <u>thing</u> that can be measured on a calendar or clock, and thus cannot possibly "fly".

However if we are referring to an older person, what is generally meant by time flying is that their lifetimes seem to becoming much more short lived.

That is because the days, months and years ahead of them no longer "creep along" but seem to excellerate and hurriedly rush forward.

On the contrary, however, when a person is quite young, he or she may feel that an endless period exists in their present and future. Indeed their future appears to be a very far off event.

Most likely this is due to the fact that young folks, for the most part, have nothing much to remember of their pasts. In fact they do not have many memorable past events as they haven't lived long enough to experience many past happenings.

But as time goes on in an older person's life, their future days on earth seem to become quite limited and therefore they are unable to contemplate longevity in the same way young people do.

Sadly older people encounter a very fast ongoing of the time they have left and thus they often say "time flies".

TIME MARCHES ON

I have no aches
I have no pain
No body change is
My refrain
And yet ...and yet
There seems to be
A little something
Wrong with me

Perhaps the answer
Truth be told
I guess indeed
I'm getting old

TOMMY TOE

You may think I am writing about a vegetable - well I am definitely not doing so. Tommy Toe was a real person - unfortunately he was very seedy and always got red in the face when exposed to the sun.

Sadly he was also extremely short and fat therefore people invariably confused him with the vegetable (or fruit as Botanists claim) that one sees in the produce departments of grocery stores.

Now Tommy Toe being a real person, always lamented the comparison made between him and a tomato, and resented being squeezed and patted when he was shopping in a produce department for himself.

Once he was even stuck on a scale (most embarrassing because he was so fat) and then almost stuffed in a brown shopping bag. He thought he was about to be included in a salad! Can you imagine? It was really terrible!

However as he got older and a little shriveled from sitting in the sun, people stopped making the comparison, so he was then quite happy, but only for a short time.

This was because his shriveling became so pronounced that he finally was mistaken for a suntried tomato and somebody sealed him in a jar and put him on a shelf in a grocery store.

The end!

TO THINK

What do the words "to think" actually mean?

Does it mean that a person is attempting to formulate an original idea in a questioning way?

Does it mean "to express an unanswerable thought in a pondering "manner"?

Does it try to convey an idea that is trying to burst through our minds?

Does it mean that our brains are working over time?

What does it actually mean?

I don't "<u>think</u>" I have the answer.

What do you <u>think</u>?

TRAYVON

Walking down the street at night
With skittles and a drink
Never knowing danger lurked
That he was on the brink
Of losing life - that death was near
A target on his chest

Followed by a pseudo cop
Who thought he was the best
And figured guns were meant to be
Used against a "black"
Regardless if he'd done no wrong
That cop's mode was "attack"!

The law said he could stand his ground
That law said lots of drivel
So Trayvon lost his precious life
In an action most "uncivil"

Oh when will laws begin to change
And guns become mere toys?
And not be used to kill or maim
Our innocent girls and boys?

TWO OF A KIND

Below is a list of similarities that exist in babies and very old people.

BABY
No teeth
Has very little hair
Eats very soft food
Is spoon fed
Hardly walks
Wears diapers
Gets wheeled around
Has nothing to remember

VERY OLD PERSON
Has dentures
Has sparse hair
Eats very soft food
Is spoon fed
Hardly walks
Wears Depends
Gets wheeled around
Forgets a lot

VACATION CLOTHES WOES

My name is Bernice Zakin and I wish to make a confession. I own a very nice apartment which includes 3 sizeable clothing closets for housing my voluminous amount of garments.

Now these articles are very lovely and are extremely fortunate. In fact they lead most pleasant lives about which I will now explain.

Each late November my sweaters and tops (the same ones from last year) are either folded neatly and placed in huge cartons, or if they are jackets and pants, they are completely covered with plastics, placed on wire hangers and hung in cardboard containers where they are tightly stuffed together, practically smothered, and then everything is carted away by a reliable moving company.

So off they go for the winter to enjoy the warm (most of the time) Florida climate.

Once in Florida they are immediately transferred to new closets and dresser drawers (neatly of course) and where they are very comfortable.

Now during the course of the winter these wearables live the good life. They go to the best restaurants and very often to the Kravis Center where they witness wonderful performers, and also meet the nicest people, plus of course they also attend lovely parties.

In fact they really live it up! for several months and never suffer a cold day.

Once in awhile they are taken to the cleaners (literally) otherwise they simply gad about town enjoying themselves. Unfortunately during the winter many of these items never see the light of day in Florida, they simply stay on their hangers and probably whisper to their fellow unchosen ones "why hasn't she picked me yet?

Sad to say, there is a very unpleasant ending to this scenario because when these articles of clothing, many of which (as I mentioned before) have never been worn during the winter, they find that on their return home to New York, there is no room in their old habitats, (i.e. their closets) due to the fact that the mean lady (me)! who supposedly took them to Florida for a lovely winter sojourn, indulged in the purchase of several new items.

Thus these old reliables found out to their dismay, that they had lost their old closet space and not only that, but in some cases, they were even being discarded!

VIEWPOINT

I just finished reading two books that were quite diverse in nature. One made me cry a copious amount of tears, that almost became actual sobs. The other convulsed me to near hysterical laughter. The first was "Me Before You" and the second was "Dad Is Fat".

I can't say which was more satisfying for me to read. I guess it depended upon my mood at the time. "Me Before You" was so poignant but the ending was probably not what the average reader would prefer and yet it was presumably inevitable.

"Dad Is Fat" on the other hand was absolutely adorable and would positively force the giggles to emerge from even the most stoic individual. It's a definite "I must read it again" volume.

So after having read both of these books I realized how fortunate I was to have found them

It is remarkable to me that the books available to us today are so unlike each other and yet have the same appeal to many different people.

We are indeed lucky to have wonderful reading matter available to all of us either in regular volume form and also on tablets.

It would be greater still if more people would take advantage of using either form of these literary endeavors.

WATER WATER EVERYWHERE

Peering down from my 23rd floor terrace I can easily track the water activities in the two swimming pools far below me.

In the smaller sized deep ended pool I can see four people (presumably men as they are bare topped) who are bobbing around like Halloween apples and although they appear to be aged and and plump, they obviously are having fun.

In the larger pool there are several ladies lapping away and doing so very ably. Indeed it's a lovely sight to behold.

Another group (mostly ladies) also seem to enjoy reclining on beach chairs hoping to end the sunny day with attractive sun tans and if I were a dermatologist I would be most pleased by their choice of recreation (it would be good for my business).

And since my high floor vantage point allows me to comfortably follow the water motions of all these swimmers and still maintain my fully clothed status, I realize how fortunate I am to just quietly watch them while lounging around on my apartment terrace chaise.

I particularly am most happy to enjoy the lovely summer weather without disrobing or getting wet!

WHAT'S IN A NAME?

Recently on one of Stephen Colbert's programs he had as a guest, a young gentleman who had just published a book presumably written as an expose of Rubert Murdock and his numerous newspaper publications throughout the world.

The book was written by Stephen's very valuable guest whose name happened to be "David Folkenflik".

Now I have a question relating to such a name. Did this person ever consider changing his name? Would the general reading public find it difficult to locate a book written by an author named Folkenflik?

I would imagine that David Folkenflik probably inherited his name from his forefathers who most likely came from a long line of Folkenfliks. But whence came they? And what did the original Folkenfliks do for a living? And how many Folkenfliks still exist? And where are they now?

These are all questions to which I would very much like valid answers. I personally never knew any Folkenfliks but I must say it would be most interesting to me if I ever met one, especially if it was David Folkenflik.

At any rate, the David Folkenflik who was Stephen Colbert's special guest would probably have the answers to my questions, but how can I possibly ever meet him?

I'm sure he is busy going on book tours throughout the country, and I do hope he is successful in selling many volumes and especially with a name like Folkenflik, I'm quite certain he should do well.

So all the best David - May your tribe increase!

Note to David:
Incidentally by any chance are you related to the Falkonflucks? If you are that would certainly be a fluke!

WHAT TO DO?

Should I stop writing? I really believe I should because at a recent party at which I celebrated my birthday, I distributed copies of my latest book to my attendees and several of them called to tell me how much they enjoyed reading it.

Now I personally know that this book was written by a not so smart or talented person (me).

Therefore those attendees (my friends) are probably not very intelligent or they would not have enjoyed said book, however if I don't stop writing they'll think I was flattered by their compliments and will keep reading my literary efforts.

On the other hand if I _do_ stop writing these same people might recognize the fact that one of us is not so smart and they might think it is a reflection upon them for liking what I write.

However if they finally realize that it is really _me_ who is not so talented, then they may not wish to associate with such a dumb person (me again) and I might lose a lot of pals.

So if I do continue writing, these friends might be hoodwinked into reading what I write and then everybody else will realize how dumb _they_ are!

WHERE DID THEY GO?

I have come to a very sad time in my life. I used to have so many lively intelligent, humorous, and fun to be with friends, but now all that seems to have changed and very suddenly.

These many people who were so involved in my life on a daily basis, have mostly disappeared but not necessarily in what I would actually term "a <u>visible</u>" way.

What happened is – they got older! And because they got older, they also developed <u>ailments</u>.

So - some are now walking with "walkers" and I don't mean the social <u>people</u> types. Some too are very busy going to doctors and therefore they have no time for <u>me</u>. Also a few are kind of "out of it" as they say.

Unfortunately too, a few have <u>died</u> so the only thing I have left of them are their obituary notices in the New York Times.

There are also a few who keep breaking dates because they forgot they made them, and still others who forgot who <u>they</u> are and who <u>I</u> am. In fact I don't know whether I should even keep a date book anymore because all my appointments keep getting scratched out.

This is really getting to be a most dreadful situation and if I could only remember what I've been writing about, I would probably be very unhappy.

WHERE DO OR DID THEY GO?

I'm now about to broach a subject which may offend many people, but I would really like to know the answer.

My question is - where do present day rabbi's put the little penis pieces they snip off after the snipping?

Do they save them? If so where? Do they send them to a storage area for future use in case of needy situations? Do they go to Israel? Are they suitable for gentile enhancement if desired?

I realize that there must be an accumulation of millions of these pieces which have been snipped through the years - indeed through the century's, therefore there has to be a place on earth huge enough to accommodate them - so where is it?

Is it possible that the answer is the Sphinx's in Egypt? Could they be partly comprised of little penis pieces? Is that the actual riddle of the Sphinx?

After all many Jewish slaves supposedly were used by the Romans to erect these constructions so it is possible that those slaves included the penis pieces during the construction period as a form of Jewish revenge.

Oy Vey! Wouldn't that be a hoot? as they say in Peoria, and how about Ozymandias? Who knows what's underneath him. He must be smiling about something special or is he a she. (Or both?!!)

At any rate there should certainly be several sizable monuments built to hold them (the penis pieces) but what country should be the beneficiary? Certainly not Germany - no doubt there are plenty of lamp shades and soap bars made from Jewish body parts from the Hitler era existing there. Therefore they don't need any extra parts.

If anyone out there has information about this puzzle. I would appreciate your enlightening me. Thank you!

WHERE IS IT ONE?

I recently heard a fleeting portion of a TV commercial which inquired as to whether I had lost my "spontaneity"

Mind you, I'm not sure if they were quizzing me personally because I was a TV listener, or were they simply interested in knowing about my possible "Joie De Vivre" or lack thereof, or perhaps the loss of my individualism or any other "ism" I might have. Then too they may have been referring to my <u>misplacement</u> of <u>something</u> more tangible or substantive.

If it was a reference to a "thing" I actually lost, I am completely unaware as to what that "thing" is or even where it might be or what it looks like.

As most of you are already aware of the huge amount of personal articles that I possess, it is entirely logical to believe that I may have inadvertently misplaced a particular item therefore "spontaneity" could possibly be one of them and <u>they</u> (whomever "they" are) may then reason that this "thing" could be anywhere. It could be in a closet or I may have left it at a friend's house,

However if they really mean to imply that my instinctive actions are missing and that I no longer have an impulsive nature nor do I do anything on a moment's notice, then I take umbrage to these insinuations, as I truly delight in following unlikely pursuits whenever I feel the urge to do so.

Therefore – Harken, to me ye television questioneers! Do not denigrate me again.

I am my own person and do as I wish whenever and wherever, particularly spontaneously.

WHERE IS IT TWO?

I think I lost it. I simply can't find it. I looked and looked in my closets and drawers even under my bed, but it positively isn't any place in my apartment.

I even called a few friends to find out if I had inadvertently left something of mine in their apartment to no avail.

So what do I do? Should I advertise in the lost and found column in my local paper? Or should I finally decide to buy a new one?

The thing is, I am not able to do that or anything else I can think of at the moment because I can't remember what it is?!!

WHICH IS HE?

What do we think about Ted Cruz? Is he fighting for our country or just for himself?

Does he want to be our President? Or just set a precedent?

How does he really think about himself? As an American? Or as a Canadian?

Does he think he is helping Republicans? Or is he a secret Democrat?

Does he consider himself just a talker? Or maybe a squawker?

Or is he simply acting "Cruzy"? Or is he really really <u>Crazy</u>!

WHINE NOT

Is it wrong to have ambition? Is it asking too much to seemingly ask for too much! Isn't America supposed to be the land of freedom, the land where success is possible for all, the land where it shouldn't matter who you are or what aspirations you have, or why these aspirations should not be fulfilled?

Am I under the delusion that I should be able to achieve my desires? I sincerely hope that this is not so because I really only want one thing....Just one!!

Actually all I want is to be part of the 1% of America, the part that is immensely wealthy that has bank accounts in many foreign countries where I would not have to pay taxes.

I would also like to have many homes (make that estates or mansions) in other places around the world so that I could cruise to them in my enormous yacht, and that it was one which might house my many friends plus an adequate staff to tend to my needs and satisfy theirs.

I don't mean to whine, nevertheless I am not of the opinion that 1% is actually such a big deal. It is a very small amount in the total scale of the American population.

So if it is at all possible, any of you out there who have the proper influence, I wish you would put in a good word for me so that I can become part of this magical 1% group.

WHO IS IT?
(A TRAGIC SITUATION!)

Shhhh! Please be very quiet. There is a person in my house whom I don't know and I have to be extremely careful to avoid that person.

Also I can never look in a mirror because that person usually creeps up behind me, and when I peek at the mirror I usually just see <u>me</u>! And that <u>me</u> is a <u>fat</u> person. Oh God! That person eats all the time! Popcorn, chips and other things that grocery people only sell to their <u>fat</u> customers.

This is a terrible dilemma to have encountered, plus the fact that my closet is also full of that <u>fat</u> person's clothing which appears to be in very <u>large sizes</u>. What shall I do?!!

"WHO LIVES IN THOSE CUTE LITTLE HOUSES"?

Many years ago when my daughter Nancy was about 3 1/2 years old, my husband and I were driving enroute to New York City, from our home in Lawrence, Long Island and passed a cemetery, whereupon Nancy queried the above statement (who lives, etc.)

This of course became her first awareness of death, which was a difficult subject to explain to a young child, nevertheless we thought she accepted it very well, but on future trips alongside the same road, she would always comment on the dead people, so who knows what she actually thought.

However just a few days ago when I again passed a cemetery, I recalled that past experience and thought to myself "who <u>does</u> live <u>under</u> those little edifices"?

I wondered whether during the "<u>dead</u>" of night (pun) there might be a visitation time for all those departed souls.

Do they actually communicate with each other? Do they discuss their pasts? Were they relatives, neighbors or good friends? Or perhaps even enemies in their former life times?

Were they happy being down under? (I don't mean Australia) or would they have preferred a different spot. Maybe under a tree or next to a different person?

Is there a certain degree of snobbishness that exists? For instance, if one person has his or her final resting place in a posh mausoleum does that bring about a feeling of envy amongst all the other <u>interred</u> individuals?

Or is it possible for any of the mausoleumed people to frown and <u>look down</u> upon the underground group? Naturally I mean figuratively, as I realize that the interred ones are <u>underneath</u> the ground as opposed to the upper crust folk in the mausoleums.

Of course when the average person is paying homage when visiting loved ones in a cemetery on birthdays, holidays or in general "let's go to see Mom, Dad, Grandpa or Grandma occasions, I don't believe he or she is thinking the thoughts I've mentioned above.

In fact I think they are probably remembering happy moments with their loved ones, or in some cases they ponder a different scenario, such as "why didn't you leave me more money than you left to my sister, brother, etc"?

At any rate visiting a cemetery is a very strange and individual experience. Some people find it comforting and peaceful, and others encounter a true sense of loss, or maybe even a spooky or eerie sensation.

But since none of us have actually returned from his or her final moments (to my knowledge), I doubt if anybody will ever be able to solve this debatable situation.

WHY WORRY

Worrying isn't very beneficial or advantageous to anyone, but nevertheless it is a very awesome and powerful thing.

It can cause a person to be anxious, fretful, unhappy, or to have many other sad and sorrowful moments.

And if I <u>personally</u> didn't worry I might be inclined to be a very happy being.

But since nobody can be happy forever, there is really no future in my being happy, although worrying certainly doesn't solve any of my problems either, therefore there is no point in worrying per se.

However every so often people speak of someone being a "worry wort", which of course has nothing to do with frogs or the worts they have or might cause, and so "worry wort" is a very silly expression.

Nevertheless, if a person did develop frog worts, that person might <u>worry</u> about how to get rid of them, which really doesn't solve anything either.

So actually we are right back to the same situation- why worry?

WINNER TAKE "HALL"

New York City is positively the most wonderful place. Where else can you find such a politically diverse group of people running for an office?

This past Mayoral race included a Jewish pervert, a white lesbian lady married to another lesbian lady, a white man married to a corn rowed black lady, with whom he has a biracial son and lastly a dark skinned individual who lost in his last bid for the same Mayoral office.

What a great choice for Gracie Mansion!

WINTER WOES

Here we are in sunny Florida, home of the kindly weatherman plus many other people who endowed this state with wonderful balmy, glorious, calm, and blue skied days.

But...and there is always a <u>but.</u> How come from outside my terrace all I can see is the constant rippling waters of the intercoastal?

Scratch that question!

Because right now I am just able to see an entire body of water which appears to be <u>pleated</u> with what I believe are really <u>wrinkles</u> and since <u>that</u> water is completely devoid of moving vessels, I actually think that this water needs some <u>Boat-Tox</u>!

WORD PROBLEMS

The other night I was sitting quietly in a comfortable chair, thinking about many innocuous things, when all of a sudden I lost "my train of thought".

So I suddenly wondered about what I had lost and what exactly was "a train of thought".

The next thing that I wondered was where did I lose it (the train of thought) and was it an actual thing or just a "figment of my imagination".

Also what did the "train" part mean? Was that something on rails? If so did it ride someplace particular in the U.S.A.? Did it have a conductor? Did it serve meals? I really didn't know.

But then I thought about the possibility of it being just "a figment of my imagination".

And if that was so - what was the "figment" Was the first part related to a fruit? But if not then I wondered what, the <u>whole</u> word "<u>figment</u>" meant. This entire situation was bothering me "no end". So then I finally solved the entire puzzle by going back to my comfortable chair to rethink comfortably. Unfortunately however I then discovered that my chair had "no end" so I wasn't very comfortable after all.

"WRITE" OR WRONG

The other day I was listening to a TV program in which all the stars of the series had received written letters from a departed member of the cast.

This gave me a great idea. I thought maybe I should do the same thing and write letters <u>too</u> after my demise. Then I would be remembered ad infinitum.

However I believed I might then encounter several obstacles if I proceeded to do this. Supposing some of my old friends moved, then I would be unable to find their new addresses.

Also having so many friends as I do, my list would then be so long that it might be impossible to write to the entire group and then some of the neglected friends might feel slighted. Besides who knows whether I'd be able to obtain stationery. Then too, what would I say, I really would not have a commonality of subjects about which to write.

My old friends would certainly have nothing in common with my dead companions, and I would not be able to relate any of my present activities to my old pals, as I wouldn't have either. (Activities or even old friends).

I then decided that being deceased would have its problems so I guess I should just "let sleeping dogs lie".

Therefore I will simply bid a final farewell to everyone when the time comes.

YOU CAN'T TAKE IT WITH YOU

I was listening to a TV program some months ago and heard someone airing a very unusual comment.

The man said he would not want to have any children, and listed the various reasons why he was against being a father.

#1. He said he liked the white meat of a chicken best and was afraid his wife to be would give that part to any children they might have, and therefore he'd be stuck with the dark meat.

#2. Also he felt he'd be responsible for spending a lot of quality time with those children, when he'd rather be enjoying himself with other pursuits.

#3. In addition he denigrated the fact that so much of his money would always be spent on expensive Christmas gifts and clothing for these kiddies, when he as their father would rather be buying these items for his own use.

You can see that he was a very selfish man indeed, and so when he suddenly passed away that December, no one came to the funeral except his butcher, accompanied by two cooked chicken breasts that he placed in the open casket.

The devoted salesman from the clothing store where the deceased always purchased his fine clothing was also present, and because the dead person left an unpaid overdue bill, the salesman, as a nice gesture placed it in the coffin as well, (of course not to be paid).

Unfortunately Santa Claus didn't get to the service because it was too close to the Christmas season and he was quite busy preparing gifts for little children.

And naturally since the man had no little kiddies none of them were there to bid him a fond farewell. (I "kid" you not!)

FINALLY – FINIS

I believe I have now come to the conclusion of my writing career.

In a way this saddens me to the utmost, not because I will regret the probable loss of inspiration, nor because I will miss using so much paper and having to buy so many pens. No, that is not what I mean at all.

What I will miss is not being able to sleep through an entire night without having to get up and write down something about which I've been thinking. Perhaps this might even be a poem I had been composing in my head and whose words I will definitely have forgotten by morning if I don't write them sometime during the night.

Mainly though I will miss my faithful readers. <u>Both</u> of them. Yes I have enjoyed having a loyal following, and I certainly will miss those <u>two</u> people.

So even though I will no longer be filling pages with words, my thoughts will always be with you <u>both</u>.

CPSIA information can be obtained at www.ICGtesting.com
Printed in the USA
BVOW07s2033031114

373488BV00001B/1/P